Glory in the Church

The Coming Revival!

Glory in the Church

The Coming Revival!

by Edward E. Hindson, Th.D.

THOMAS NELSON INC., PUBLISHERS

New York/Nashville

Copyright © 1975 by Edward E. Hindson.
All rights reserved under International and Pan-American
Conventions
Published by Thomas Nelson, Inc., Nashville, Tennessee
Manufactured in the United States of America

Library of Congress Cataloging in Publication Data

Hindson, Edward E.
  Glory in the church.
  1. Revivals.   I. Title.

BV3790.H48   269′.2   75-17883
ISBN 0-8407-5600-3 pbk.

"Now unto Him that is able to do exceeding
abundantly above all that we ask or think,
according to the power that worketh in us,
unto Him be *Glory in the Church*
by Christ Jesus throughout all ages,
world without end, Amen."
(EPHESIANS 3:20-21)

contents

PREFACE   xi

1. Revival: Glory in the Church   15

2. Nature of Genuine Revival   26

3. Obstacles to Revival   41

4. The Holy Spirit Gives Revival   54

5. Prayer: The Power of Revival   64

6. Neglected Doctrines of Revival:
   Repentance and the Lordship of Christ   73

7. Revival Preaching and Crusades   91

8. Counseling and Revival   105

   Postscript: "The Story of the Lynchburg Revival"
   by Dr. Jerry Falwell   118

preface

This book deals with revival in the church. The term "revival" is one of the most misunderstood and misused of all ecclesiastical terms. To some, it is equated with irrational emotionalism. To others, it is a term of the distant past (generally replaced with a more acceptable term like "renewal"). Still others look upon revival with heartwarming nostalgia as something that was good for the past but will never again be experienced.

The American intoxication with technology and materialism has caused us to lapse into a "post-Christian" immoralism. Public officials refuse to use the word "sin"; prayer has been banned from our schools; and biblical morality is looked upon as a psychological misfortune, "obsolete" and "medieval." Our national quest for intellectual credibility and our scientific computerization of proper "methods" have not only affected our civil life, but our churches as well. However, the intellectual pursuits and methodological approaches of the church have failed to bring any real or lasting revival.

Thus, the content of this book seeks no intellectual acceptance (there are no footnotes, though a previous book of mine had 373) and no new methods are offered. Instead, the reader will find a simple scriptural study of revival and some of its essential (but rarely used) elements: repentance, prayer, and discipleship.

Very few worthwhile books have ever been written on the topic of revival. Some, unfortunately, have been written by people who have never experienced one. This book follows the basic outline of Dr. Robert Sprague, whose *Lectures on Revival* (1832) are among the finest available. This godly Calvinistic Presbyterian of the nineteenth century lived during several great revival eras. His comments are solid, practical, and well worth reading.

The approach of the present study also relates a vivid account of an actual modern day revival. In the "Postscript" by Dr. Jerry Falwell, you will be able to read for yourself the events of the revival at Lynchburg, Virginia, in October, 1973. This account should be adequate evidence that the size of a church is no hinderance to revival.

A brief word needs to be said about the style and approach of this book. You will find several *direct appeals* to the reader. This method, used very effectively over the centuries, has almost disappeared from literature. You will also find several repetitious phrases, such as the term "genuine." This is done deliberately because of the great need to emphasize continually the reality of true revival as opposed to false concepts of it. May your reading of this book open heaven's windows of blessing and stir your heart to revival.

A word of acknowledgement and appreciation for helpful suggestions is due Dr. Jerry Falwell, pastor of the Thomas Road Baptist Church in Lynchburg, Virginia, and to Rev. Del Fehsenfeld, Jr., director of Life Action Crusades of St. Petersburg, Florida. Together they share the great burden for revival in America in our lifetime. A word of appreciation ought to go also to Mrs. Margaret McCoy who graciously corrected and typed the original manuscript.

Edward E. Hindson, Th.D.
Lynchburg, Virginia
October, 1974

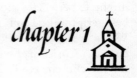

chapter 1

Revival: "Glory" in the Church!

"Unto him be glory in the church by Christ Jesus throughout all ages, world without end. Amen."
(EPHESIANS 3:21)

A famous Scottish theologian remarked that no one living in the English speaking world and born after World War I, has ever witnessed a genuine revival! Jesus promised: "I will build my church; and the gates of hell shall not prevail against it" (Matt. 16:18). Throughout twenty centuries of church history, He has been doing just that. The messengers of Christ have taken His gospel to virtually every corner of the globe. The Lord of the church has developed, sanctified, chastised, and cleansed His church over and over again.

Strangely, while God has visited America with revival in both the eighteenth and nineteenth centuries, there has never been a genuine nationwide revival in Amrica during the twentieth century! Yet, this is the era of bigger churches and mass-communication systems that flash the message of Christ across the nation and around the world. Have we taken the wrong approach, or are we merely preparing for a genuine outburst of revival which shall yet come?

The apostle Paul prayed that the Ephesian church

15

might experience "glory in the church." This is the best scriptural definition of revival that one can find. When revival comes, it results in "glory in the church." Christ died, not only for individuals, but also for the church. He is coming again, not just for individuals, but for His church. When He sovereignly brings revival to the church, He is "glorified in His saints."

What is "glory in the church?" It is visible through the lives of God's people. When there is "glory" in the church, the people hunger and thirst after righteousness, their hearts are aflame with service to God, and their community is affected by an outburst of soul-winning activity. No one must prod the revived congregation to obey God. No one need threaten the glorified church into serving the Saviour. The fruit of obedience is evidence enough that God is at work in His church.

How can one tell if there is "glory in the church?" The glory of God is more than the brightness of heaven. God's glory is the radiance of His very deity and is always synonymous with His presence. Wherever God is, there His glory is manifest. Moses claimed to see the glory of God. So did Isaiah and Ezekiel. What did they actually see? They beheld the radiance of the very presence of God. What is "glory in the church?" It is the very presence of God actively at work among His people. Just as the glory of God filled the holy of holies in Israel, His glory fills the revived church.

This book is a study of that "glory" which is revival in the church. In order to comprehend better the terminology of this study, we need to give some basic definitions.

Revival: a renewed sense of zeal among Christians causing them to obey God more fervently.

Evangelism: proclaiming the salvation message of the gospel to the unsaved.

Awakening: a general stirring among all of society (saved and unsaved) which calls attention to God's activity within the church.

Why No Revival?

At the present time there is a great deal of confusion as to the difference between revival and evangelism. Both are essential works of God among His people. However, they remain two totally different functions. Revival causes the Christian to look *inward* and search his own heart, whereas evangelism causes him to look *outward* toward those needing the Saviour. Many evangelistic meetings are improperly labeled "revival" meetings. All the preaching is to the lost. While this is needed, it has often been done to the neglect of preaching righteousness to the saved.

The major human reason for our not experiencing genuine revival in the twentieth century is twofold: 1) Christians have failed to meet the conditions of revival (2 Chron. 7:14); 2) However, they have failed because of a lack of genuine revival preaching. The ultimate blame must come back to the pulpit. Very few preachers and evangelists are proclaiming the righteousness of Christian living to God's people. All too often, we have turned our church invitations into a "spectator sport" in which the Christians "peek" to see who is so terrible that they need to "go forward." In many fundamental churches it has almost come to the point that it is a crime ever to have responded publicly in a service!

There is also a further underlying factor that has squelched twentieth century revival in the Western world. While we have gone without a fresh visitation from God, other parts of the world have been stirred afresh by the Lord of the church: Korea, Indonesia, and Africa. In fact, America has been without revival for so long that many fundamentalists refuse to believe that these other nations have really experienced revival. Their attitude has taken the pharisaical opinion: "If I cannot have it, then neither can you."

Will the Drought Last Forever?

Some have even gone so far as to say there will *never* be another real revival. They say it is too late for America, for we are in the "Laodicean Church Age." God cannot revive an apostate church, and we are in the "age of apostasy." Thus, they rationalize away all hope for revival. Man is an unusual creature. Whenever he has not seen something happen and cannot seem to make it happen, he will always conclude that "it cannot happen." This is the very same attitude that said man would never get to the moon. When the astronauts landed, there were still some who refused to believe it!

There are great dangers in saying there will never be another revival:

1. Throughout church history, every religious group (denomination or faction) who took this view ended up opposing real revival when it did come. History has proven that those groups which opposed revival in the past were always

bypassed by the working of God in His church. *They* lapsed into apostasy!

2. That it is too late for revival to come to America is based upon a false interpretation of Revelation 3:14-19. This false assumption is that the Laodicean Church is the church of the last period of church history and is, therefore, the twentieth century church. This conjecture remains to be proven, as does the entire "system" of identifying the seven churches of Revelation with the "periods" of church history.

Notice, first of all, that the Laodicean Church was a specific *local church* in Asia Minor. It was not an apostate church. It still had a "candlestick", and Jesus said of this church: "As many as I *love,* I rebuke and chasten: be zealous therefore, and repent" (Rev. 3:19). In fact, the description of this church sounds like a lot of today's fundamental churches! ". . . Thou sayest, I am rich, and increased with goods, and have need of nothing; and knowest not that thou art wretched, and miserable, and poor, and blind, and naked" (Rev. 3:17).

Secondly, notice the instruction given to this lukewarm church which Jesus (though grieved) still loved. "I counsel thee to buy of me *gold* tried in the fire, that thou mayest be rich; and *white raiment,* that thou mayest be clothed, and that the shame of thy nakedness do not appear; and anoint thine eyes with *eyesalve,* that thou mayest see" (Rev. 3:18). The instruction here, though symbolized, is obvious. Each depicts righteousness: gold, righteousness of character; white raiment, righteousness of life; eyesalve, righteousness of vision.

What is the message to the Laodicean

Church? "Be zealous therefore, and repent" (Rev. 3:19). This is always the message of Christ to the unrevived church. Dead orthodoxy always results in lukewarm practice. Nowhere in this passage is this church reprimanded for heresy, but for spiritual poverty. If there is a modern Laodicean Church, it is the fundamental church with its self-sufficient, self-righteous complacency! Begin to preach righteousness and repentance to this church, and revival will result! This is not the liberal and apostate church, for they have no candlestick! Begin to preach that *your church* is in danger of becoming the Laodicean Church, and see what God does!

3. The attitude that revival cannot come in our time is contrary to this very statement in Ephesians: "Unto him be glory in the church by Christ Jesus *throughout all ages,* world without end. Amen (Eph. 3:21). It is the purpose of God to bring glory into the church in every age. Twentieth century revival is a reality in the church in other lands, and it can be in America and England as well.

Sounds from Heaven

Every great revival has been characterized by new "sounds from heaven." A heaven-sent, Holy Ghost empowered revival cannot be mistaken for something shallow and man-made. We need to hear from heaven today as the church did at Pentecost. We need heaven-sent sermons bathed in prayer and empowered by God to bring conviction to the sleeping church.

Revival among the saved will always result in an outburst of evangelism among the lost. Evangelism is the automatic byproduct of revival. One may prod an unrevived congregation to soul-winning activity with gifts and gimmicks, but such prodding is unnecessary in the revived church.

When the New Testament Christians "heard from heaven", the message they caught "sounded out from them" throughout the world. God has promised: "If *my* people, which are called by my name, shall *humble* themselves, and *pray,* and *seek my face,* and *turn from their wicked ways;* then will I hear from heaven, and will forgive their sin, and will heal their land" (2 Chron. 7:14). Our nation is in desperate need of a healing and cleansing touch from God. We need to hear from Him. He is merely waiting to hear from us! Why do we not pray as we ought? Why will we not humble ourselves and seek His face? Because we are not willing to "turn from our wicked ways." Herein is the key to revival. God's people must be convicted of *their sin,* repent, and hear again from heaven.

C. H. Spurgeon once called his nation to a revival of:

1. powerful preaching
2. old-fashioned doctrine
3. fervent prayer
4. personal godliness
5. domestic (family) devotions
6. genuine love

One of the major reasons that revival never continued into the twentieth century was the rise of "liberalism" in theology. As liberalism spread through the major denominations during the early twentieth century, it was obvious that the revivals of the nineteenth century were over. Genuine revival always brings with it purity of doctrine and purity of life. When the church is not experiencing revival, heresy of doctrine will always creep in and be tolerated.

During the fundamentalist-liberal controversies of the early decades of this century, the church defended herself against attack from within. The intense doctrinal focus which followed was necessary to preserve the truth from virtual annihilation. As Dr. Machen so ably noted at the time, "liberalism" was not a new form of Christianity. It was not Christianity at all! It was another religion devoid of biblical truth.

In time the intense concentration upon the liberal controversy swung the church's attention away from revival. Battle lines were drawn and redrawn. Despite what appeared to be initial success upon the part of the liberals, God ultimately vindicated the true church. Today, while liberalism is failing and dying, fundamental Christianity is prospering. Conservative, independent churches are the largest and fastest growing in America. Still there has been no lasting outburst of revival in our time.

Church History Is the History of Revival

The only eras of church history that are really worth studying with satisfaction are those periods when the church was in revival. The highlights of the Christian church are its revival movements. When we stop patting ourselves on the back, as if we alone are righteous and faithful, and begin to see ourselves as God sees us, we will have revival. We have fought the enemy effectively. Let us stop fighting with the "friends of the gospel" and pray for a manifestation of God's glory within the true church.

The blame for the lack of revival during the early twentieth century must be laid at the feet of the liberals, not the fundamentalists who sought to defend the truth. Liberalism swung the focus of spiritual attention away from revival and placed it upon survival. The fundamental church has indeed survived. However, when engaged in battle, one may develop a "fighting mentality" and after defeating the opponent, he may continue to fight with everyone else in sight!

Certain essential facts are prominent in the history of revival. First, revival has rarely come during a time of controversy, but rather during a time of lethargy. Whenever the church seemed most dismal and powerless, Christ has sent the Holy Spirit upon the church in an unusual manner. Every revival in church history has been instantaneous and humanly inexplicable in that it came when least expected. Controversy often developed during the revival (see Luther, Wesley, Edwards, and Whitefield), but was rarely the actual cause of it.

Secondly, revival has usually come as the result of a renewed emphasis upon a neglected scriptural doctrine and a new zealousness in prayer. Dr. Plumer, in the introduction to his commentary on the book of Romans, claims that every major revival may be traced back to a fresh recapturing of the powerful soteriological doctrines of Romans.

Thirdly, revival movements tend to unite the efforts of genuinely reborn Christians, while being opposed by mere professing "Christians." When revival comes, it will bring a sense of spiritual unity to God's

Revival: Glory in the Church   23

people and will reveal the real "enemies" of the cross.

A fourth feature of revival is that it comes without denominational distinction (whether we want it to or not)! God is concerned about His people, and Christ's love is toward His church no matter what their denominational label. Even the most ardent Calvinist must admit to the blessings of God upon Wesley and Finney. The strongest Arminian would not deny the power of God in the revivals of Edwards and Whitefield, or in the ministry of Spurgeon.

A final and sobering fact of revival history is that every major revival came during a time of peace and was followed by war. When God had finished preparing His church for what lay ahead, and when those who rejected His work had confirmed their unbelief, revival would end and war would come. Notice but a few examples:

> Great Awakening (1734-74); Revolutionary War began 1776.
> Revival of 1805 (1805-09); War of 1812.
> Great Prayer Revival (1857-59); Civil War began 1860.

What lies ahead for our nation? The wars and natural catastrophies of the "great tribulation" certainly shall come. Undoubtedly, the rise of the false religious system of the anti-Christ has already begun. Yet, all of this in no way eliminates the possibility of revival in the twentieth century. What a glorious experience to see a "Third Great Evangelical Awakening" prior to the coming of Christ for His church.

Jesus is coming to help His church of which He said: "The gates of hell shall not prevail against it" (Matt. 16:18). Oh that we might see this church as militant, superaggressive, and revived: a prepared bride awaiting her prince from glory! Let us not be content with a weak and cowering church, helplessly pleading for the rapture to spare us. Recapture the biblical cry of the church: not a defenseless "help", but a triumphant, ". . . Even so, come, Lord Jesus" (Rev. 22:20). We must be revived and ready to meet the Saviour with that glorious response. This, then, is "glory in the church!"

chapter 2 🏠

Nature of Genuine Revival

"Drop down, ye heavens, from above, and let the skies pour down righteousness: let the earth open, and let them bring forth salvation, and let righteousness spring up together; . . ." (ISAIAH 45:8)

Genuine revival has always been the method through which the outpouring of the Spirit of God has come upon the church. Through the ages of church history, time and time again God has moved to bless His church in a very wonderful way. Revival came through the ministry of the apostles, the "post-apostolic" preachers, the reformers, and then the great men of God that were used in the subsequent centuries to proclaim the gospel. In the history of American Christianity, our nation experienced genuine, nationwide revival in the eighteenth century, and again in the nineteenth century. The first "Great Awakening" and the second "Evangelical Awakening" were by far the greatest religious movements of their time. Through the moving of God in revival, the course of our nation's moral life was directly influenced by heaven. Revivals of the great Puritan preachers, such as Jonathan Edwards and later the revival influence of George Whitefield and others, brought our nation back to her knees and back to

God. However, we have never seen such a sweeping revival in the twentieth century.

What Is Revival?

The question that needs to be clarified in each of our minds is: "What is the nature of genuine revival?" If it is our honest desire to see revival, to see this nation moved by God in a Third Great Evangelical Awakening before the coming of Christ, for what are we looking? We must begin with a scriptural definition of the term "revival." More than anything else, revival consists in the conformity of the heart and life to the will of God. It involves the principle of obedience implanted in the soul, and then the operation of that principle in the conduct of the individual. In the latter part of he twentieth century, the church needs, more than ever, a new zeal and determination to obey the principles of the Word of God. The permissive society, of which we are all a part, has tended to so conform and deform our own attitudes and concepts toward Godly living, that what we consider to be the best of Christian living is often far inferior to the standards of the Word of God.

Genuine revival must, first of all, involve an increase of zeal and devotion in the lives of God's people. When Christians are awakened to a realization of their neglected obligations, their unconfessed sin, their unfaithfulness in serving Christ, they will then begin to appropriate the grace of God as never before in their daily lives. Confessing their sin, failure, and needs, they will begin to gain a deeper sense of humility and call out for the genuine working of God in their lives.

This increase in zealousness to live for Christ moves them to cry for the descent of the Holy Spirit upon those around them, upon the church of which they are a member, on their friends who are living at some distance from God, on all of those who are outside the experience of salvation. Their conversation becomes predominantly more spiritual, more edifying, and more Christ-centered. Their life pattern begins to revolve around a genuine spiritual relationship with God. The self-centered, half-hearted indifference that so commonly predominates the church is swept aside by a new and genuine desire to live for God in earnestness and power. The general course of one's life is no longer centered around the selfish pursuit of pleasure and personal gratification, but rather radiates around a renewed interest in glorifying God.

Revival Now or Never!

Jesus foresaw the church as militant, aggressive, and always attacking the gates of hell (Matt. 16:18). He never saw His church as a weark and defenseless organization cowering under the threat of Satan and the ungodly world system in which it had to exist. Instead, He saw the church literally attacking the very gates of hell, which would not be able to stand up against the onslaught of the church. Today much of this concept has changed. Instead of genuinely singing "Onward, Christian soldiers marching as to war," all too often we act as if we are saying: "Walk softly, Christian soldier, step in doubt and fear, with the cross of Jesus dragging up the rear!" Instead of marching out of our churches with a renewed zeal and desire to reach a world that needs the Saviour, we march off to the local restaurant and fill our stomachs with an excessive amount of food. We become sleepy, lazy, indifferent, and go home to our oppulent affluence, and bathe in the indifference of materialism!

Revival begins to renew the viewpoint and value system of the Christian. It brings a renewed realization of the statement of Jesus, "You cannot serve God and mammon" (materialism). No man can serve two masters" (Matt. 6:24). The Word of God makes that clear. Yet, the general experience of the average Christian today is an attempt to do this very thing: to hold to Christ and the world, to mix religion and Christianity with worldliness, compromise, and outright sinfulness. The result is the miserable, lukewarm condition of a modern Laodicean Church!

A definite feature of genuine revival is a sense of deep conviction among previously careless Christians. Those who have been indifferent and careless to the claims of Christ are suddenly more seriously moved and convicted to realize the statement of the Word of God: ". . . Let every one that nameth the name of Christ depart from iniquity" (2 Tim. 2:19). God has called His people to be a holy and righteous people. Holiness should always characterize the people of God, and yet holiness is the one thing that does not characterize God's people today! Worldiness, carelessness, and indifference characterize them, but not a genuine hunger for righteousness. In the Sermon on the Mount, Jesus made it clear that those who were genuinely saved would "hunger and thirst after righteousness." In your Christian experience, what do you hunger for, what do you thirst after, what is the longing of your soul? Is there a longing desire to be more like Christ? Or in reality, is the longing of your soul that the pastor would not preach so long on Sunday morning, nor extend the invitation to the length that he does!

When geniune revival is sent by God to a church, those who have once disdained the things of God and taken lightly their commitment and responsibility to the Lord, are now moved with a deep and genuine sense of conviction (Acts 8:21-22). They begin to realize, for the first time perhaps, that all sin is an offense to a holy and righteous God. They realize that God will hold them accountable, not only for every action, but even for every idle word (Matt. 12:36)! It is this sense of conviction that turns one to gènuine repentance (2 Cor. 7:10). Repentance is an attitude of the heart that says, in essence, "Lord, anything you show me to be sin now, and anything you reveal to me in the future to be sin, I will give up for you." Some do not like the terminology of "total surrender," but acknowledgment of Christ has always involved an absolutely unconditional surrender to the Lordship of Christ (Acts 9:5-6).

Our churches are overloaded with claiming "Christians" who do not live the evidence of their profession. These so-called converts of "believe-only" evangelism have become the biggest heartache of the church. They must constantly be prodded to live the kind of life that they are totally incapable of producing. Christian life conferences do not cause them to live a genuine Christian life; soul winning seminars do not make soul winners of them. They are the "dead wood" of the church. Religiously, they merely exist without the reality of regeneration.

Almost Is Not Enough!

As God begins to move in genuine revival, there

are always those who are (in the terminology of the last century) only "partially awakened." These are the type people who partially repent. They have an incomplete experience of repentance. In essence, they look on and see what is happening and are moved with a sense of concern for revival. They acknowledge God's agency in it, and, at times, manifest a feeling of respect toward it, and even express a desire to experience more of it. They may attend the services more regularly, they may be pleased with the results, they may observe the entire matter with a great sense of respect and seriousness; but, after all this, they genuinely do not come to a decisive point of repentance, or even to a true conviction of sin. These "half-hearted" Christians are the most heartbreaking of all. They, coming so close to the truth and yet falling so far short of it, become the most difficult of all to reach. They certainly "have a form of godliness but deny the power thereof" (2 Tim. 3:5).

Opposition to Revival

There is also the group who openly criticize and often condemn genuine revival. Locked in their selfish pursuit of sin, they are unaccustomed to a sense of geniune conviction among God's people. Therefore, they are often embarrassed and made uncomfortable during a time of geniune revival. They are hesitant even to attend such meetings, and excuse their own lack of spiritual interest with a shallow, "intellectual," rationalization of their sin. However, we need to be reminded that whenever one faces scoffing and violent opposition, he may note that those people are usually under a sense of genuine conviction.

Those who are totally indifferent to the claims of Christ and the working of God are the most spiritually destitute of all. Many times, those who violently oppose the work of God and openly blaspheme God, condemning even the statements of the Word of God, are under a deep sense of guilt and conviction, which they are desperately trying to suppress and sublimate in their own conscience. It has been the experience of Christians over the centuries to discover that many of these hostile opponents of the gospel are often brought to genuine conversion. The scriptural example could begin with the apostle Paul.

Genuine conviction of sin must always precede true revival. An excellent scriptural example may be found in the revivals under Hezekiah, Josiah, and Nehemiah. For example, as the people of Israel rebuilt the walls of Jerusalem in Nehemiah's time, they came under deep conviction from the reading of the law. In Nehemiah 8, Ezra, the scribe, read the book of the law of Moses to the assembled nation before the Water Gate.

Ezra and the Levites ". . . read in the book in the law of God distinctly, and gave the sense, and caused them to understand the reading" (Neh. 8:8): The impact of this personal confrontation with the righteous standards of God broke the peoples' hearts. ". . . For all the people wept, when they heard the words of the law" (Neh. 8:9). Ezra continued to read the Word of God to the assembled nation for seven days. They declared a national fast and repentance (Neh. 9:1). The people separated themselves from all strangers and came unto the Lord and confessed their sins before Him.

How unlike the "Watergate Cover-up Incident" in our nation! These Israelites listened to the Word of God one fourth of a day and confessed their sins one fourth of a day before the Water Gate in Jerusalem. Revival is never obtained by ignoring or covering sin. The Psalmist declared, "The Lord is nigh unto them that are of a broken heart; and saveth such as be of a contrite spirit" (Ps. 34:18).

The Nature of True Revival

Since revival has been so long awaited by the twentieth century church, and since we have experienced such a dearth of genuine Christian commitment and living in the latter part of this century, many people do not understand the nature of true revival. Therefore, many false concepts of revival are in existence today. Often one will drive past a church advertising "revival services," but the services being conducted are not revival services at all! They are, rather, evangelistic services or "Christian-life" services. The tag of "revival" has been placed on many extraneous activities of twentieth century "churchianity" to the point that many have often failed to catch even a glimpse of genuine Heaven-sent revival. However, there are some definite qualities found in a true revival.

1. *Revival is more than excitement.* When God is moving on His church in a special way to call His people to conviction of sin and to a new determination to obey His Word, that movement will always gain the attachment of a sense of genuine excitement. But excitement itself is not necessarily an evidence of true revival. Many times, by the means of artificial stimulae, man has been able to conjure up a great deal of excitement over religious activity, which is unscriptural, unseparated, and unsanctified.

The enthusiasm and excitement of many churches

and youth groups may appear attractive; and yet, the excitement which they promote is, all too often, self-produced, self-induced, and short-lived in the reality of its experience. The wildest reveries of fanaticism have been labeled by some as "revival." The emotional excessiveness of a "holy roller" expression of Christianity has often carried with it the stamp of confusion, irreverence, and impiety. One genuinely cannot put the seal of approval of the Holy Spirit on man-made excitement which lacks genuine scriptural truth and the clear expression of godly living.

Revival is much more than excitement. Church history has proven that true revival may be calm, and even noiseless. Multitudes of hearts have been broken in contrition and in yielding to God; yet, they have never experienced convulsive emotions in the expression of that conviction. It is true that in most instances of genuine revival, the Spirit of God does move the hearts of His people to an honest and sincere expression of emotion. However, that expression comes as a result of the conviction of sin, not as a result of psychological stimulae that are merely man-made.

2. *Revival is more than "Decisions."* Probably today, as never before in the history of the church, we are inclined to attribute "decisions" as the evidence of revival. Extreme emphasis on the free will of man has brought contemporary fundamentalism to the point of "decisionalism" and "easy-believism." The convicted sinner is quickly given a three or four-step process by which he may in a matter of one or two minutes totally repent of sin, turn to God, and be born into the family of God. While conversion is instantaneous, it ought not to be taken too lightly, quickly, or cheaply.

More "decisions" are being recorded today in evangelistic crusades than ever before in the history of the church, and yet we are not experiencing genuine revival! There is less conviction of sin, less zeal to obey the principles of the Word of God, and less of a concern for genuine, godly living. Why? Many of these "decisions" are the result of people believing in Christ in the sense that a child would believe in Santa Claus. These responses lead to the unscriptural statement: "Let's pray that these decisions will stick." If one is genuinely saved, the experience of regeneration is the result of the new birth produced by the Spirit of God (John 3:5-6). When one is regenerated or born again by the power of the Holy Spirit, his "decision" will certainly "stick" for all eternity! One need not pray that a decision "stick" when the person is genuinely saved, but the weakness of our presentation of the gospel and the ineffective lives of those who are supposedly "converted" have resulted in such unscriptural concepts and practices that are prevalent among some fundamentalists.

The proof that "decisions" alone are not the result of genuine revival is the stark reality of the fact that a large percentage of those making "decisions" finally fall away, proving the entire work that produced them to be spurious. Genuine revival will always produce genuine results (John 15:5). Man-made religious attempts, even when bathed in the terminology and practice of "fundamentalism," will always fall into disrepute. It is no secret that when "converts" of the average mass evangelistic campaign of the twentieth century are followed up, only a minute percentage show any evidence of sincere Christian living. When God moves in true revival, there will always be great numbers genuinely converted! The immediacy of decision, however, does not necessarily prove the reality of revival. Proof lies in the genuine continuance of those who come to the Saviour. It is obvious that if the genuineness of revival is to be determined, it must be determined on the quality of its professed subjects.

3. *Persecution is not always proof of revival.* Since the carnal mind is at enmity with Christ (Rom. 8:7), it will always be in direct opposition to the work of God. Genuine revival has always been opposed throughout the history of the church. Nothing did more to weaken the church in America in the nineteenth century than the opposition to the revival under Whitefield. Those who are not moved by revival, especially when it involves the genuine conviction of sin, will always tend to oppose it and justify their own indifference. But despite this obvious truth, opposition alone does not prove the reality of revival. The opposition most often complained of, or even gloried in by various preachers, is not to the truth contained in the Word of God, but rather, to the harsh and irritating expressions of that truth, namely, the idiosyncracies of the preacher's personality. Instead of suffering for righteousness' sake, these men, all too often, are "buffeted for their own faults!"

Revival: The Real Thing!

Genuine revival must be the result of the working of God. Whatever God produces will bear the stamp of His approval. Therefore, in order to understand the true nature of revival, one must understand the source of genuine revival.

1. *Revival comes by scriptural means.* God has given us His Word not only as a rule of faith, but

also of practice. In the same proportion that we adhere to it, we have a right to expect His blessing; and in the same proportion that we depart from it, we have a reason to expect His frown. God will always honor His Word (Isa. 55:11). When the proclamation of the gospel and the practice of Christian living are consistently in line with the principles of the Word of God, one can expect genuine revival. Such revival cannot come by unscriptural means, although, in our day, tremendous excitement, religious zeal, and interest have been produced by unscriptural doctrines and unscriptural means.

Because religious leaders often face a desperate lack of spiritual power and a lack of revival, they will always be tempted to substitute a mass of machinery designed to psychologically effect the passions of man. When this happens, Christianity loses its qualities of genuine repentance, faith, and holiness; it retreats into an emotional experience where people fall, groan, and shout. Genuine revival is not mere emotionalism, nor is it mere intellectualism. Revival of God's people must come through the simple and honest prescriptions of the Word of God for their lives (1 John 3:22). When one has proclaimed the truth contained in the Word of God and practiced His teachings, he can reasonably expect his ministry to be characterized by the genuine work of the Holy Spirit.

2. *Revival comes with conviction of sin.* Remorse, contrition, and confession of sin are the results of the work of the Holy Spirit. While the unsaved should sincerely be offered the gospel, they must understand and accept genuine separation from worldliness as the core of Christian living. A deepening conviction of sin must first begin in the lives of reborn Christians.

When they have surrendered their selfishness and sinfulness through confession, God will begin to move on them (2 Chron. 7:14). The world is waiting to see whether professed Christians are really serious about their relationship to the living God.

Although preaching repentance has always held an important position in the scriptures, it has been neglected in our time. This neglect is the major reason why believers, as well as unbelievers, have no conviction about the reality of sin. "For godly sorrow worketh repentance to salvation . . ." (2 Cor. 7:10). Genuine revival results in thorough conviction when people are truly distressed over their sin. Sorrow for sin precedes complete repentance.

The Word of God, with its laws and standards, must confront the sinner with the reality of his offense and the severity of God's anger which he deserves for his sin. A glimpse of this awful truth brings the kind of sorrow that results in repentance and salvation.

Genuine revival will come only when there is a genuine conviction of sin. The entertainment-oriented evangelism of the twentieth century has fallen short of revival at this very point!

3. *Revival results in substantial and abiding fruit.* In 1 Cor. 14:25-25, we read of God's ultimate form of evangelism in the church: "But if all prophesy, and there come in one that believeth not, or one unlearned, he is convinced of all, he is judged by all: and thus are the secrets of his heart made manifest; and so falling down on his face he *will worship God,* and *report that God is in you* of a truth." The proclamation of the gospel must be accompanied by the sincere and serious lives of godly people. Their very lives reinforce the testimony of the message. They are living examples of God's truth.

The apostle Paul makes it clear in this passage that godly, fruit-bearing Christians are used by the Holy Spirit to convince the unbeliever of his sin. Our churches, however, are at such a point of spiritual despair that the unsaved feel comfortable and "at home" in them. Many churches revolve around a program and personnel that are so worldly that the unbeliever could not possibly see God at work in their lives.

When one's conversion is produced by the regeneration of the Holy Spirit, his life will automatically produce spiritual fruit (John 15:16). The nine fruits of the Spirit, listed in Galatians 5:22-23, are not given as mere options for the Christian life. They are the immediate product of a new life (2 Cor. 5:17). Jesus made it clear that some believers would product fruit a hundredfold, some sixtyfold, some thirtyfold (Matt. 13:8). Notice, however, that He gave none the choice of whether to produce fruit or not. No fruit? No life!

When many who profess to have been converted during a "revival" meeting return to the world and to careless and ungodly living, they give evidence to the shallowness and weakness of that so-called "revival." Their conduct proves that it was a revival produced by men, not by God. If the revival genuinely came from the Spirit of God, the virtues and graces of Christ-likeness should adorn the lives of those who profess to be converted.

The fruit of vegetation is the result of plant germination. The fruit of human reproduction is the result of marriage. Notice carefully the words of Romans 7:4, "Wherefore, my brethren, ye also are become dead to the law by the body of Christ; that ye should be *married* to another, even to him who is raised from the dead, that we should bring forth *fruit* unto

God." Union with Christ results in a new and fruitful life. Revival, if it is to be judged as coming from God, must result in substantial and abiding fruit.

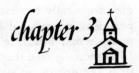

chapter 3

Obstacles to Revival

"Others mocking said, These men are full of new wine." (ACTS 2:13)

". . . lest we should hinder the gospel of Christ." (1 CORINTHIANS 9:12)

No one more than the apostle Paul endured such hardships for the sake of the gospel. "Satan hindered us," he often proclaimed. Genuine revival always faces basic obstacles. Once these are overcome by the Holy Spirit, the will of God may be accomplished in the lives of His people.

Is the Pastor to Blame?

Believe it or not, the pastor is often the major hindrance to revival in the church. Pastor, your heart must be moved to revival before God will move the hearts of your people. You must desire the outpouring of the Spirit. You must be willing to let God deal with sin in your life. Some ministers do not desire the experience of genuine revival because they know that revival will cost them *their* sin.

Other pastors may hinder revival simply because

they are totally ignorant of true revival. Their temperament, educational background, and religious experience may influence their attitudes toward revival. It is especially true that in the latter part of the twentieth century many pastors have never witnessed a genuine revival. Therefore, they tend to label certain experiences as "revival" which are not true revivals at all. Other pastors have become so insensitive to revival that they would not be able to recognize it if they did see it!

The skeptics and critics of revival are like those who "see it but never taste of it." They are merely spectators, not recipients, of God's blessings. Like the captain of the king's guard, they refuse to acknowledge the hand of God's blessing. In 2 Kings 6:24–7:20, we read of the prophet Elisha's announcement that famine-stricken, beseiged Samaria would overflow with an abundance of food overnight. The captain mockingly replied, ". . . Behold, if the Lord would make windows in heaven, might this thing be?" To which, Elisha answered, ". . . Thou shalt see it with thine eyes, but shalt not eat thereof" (2 Kings 7:2). The very next day, as the starved people rushed in and out of the city for the food which God had provided, the captain was trampled to death in the gate of Samaria. Truly, he saw God's miracle, but he never tasted of it!

God is looking for spiritual "soldiers," not spectators. Pastor, your attitudes may very well determine whether your people will be visited afresh by God. The message of revival is for you, not just for your people. "Search me, O God, and know my heart; try me, and know my thoughts: and see if there be any wicked way in me, and lead me in the way everlasting" (Ps. 139:23-24).

Can a Man Serve Two Masters?

A spirit of worldliness among professed Christians is the greatest hindrance to the genuine moving of God in a revival. Today's Christian often reveals too much concern for the things of this world. One of the greatest problems of the church is that, all too often, Christians actually envy the world! On the one hand, we claim that we are thrilled to be saved. We testify to the greatness of the joy of salvation. Yet, on the other hand, we still look back longingly on the very sins from which we have been saved.

This condition is often the result of "decisions" made by those who desire to be saved from hell and its punishments, but who do not really desire to be saved from sin. For that reason, they tend to look longingly upon their sinful past, still desiring to make sin a part of their present experience. Like Lot's wife, they are about to become a pillar of salt! The result is frustration in trying to serve God and the world too. Jesus said that you cannot love God and love the world. "No man can serve two masters: for either he will hate the one, and love the other; or else he will hold to the one, and despise the other. Ye cannot serve God and mammon" (Matt. 6:24).

The church may be hampered by the materialistic desires of the average Christian who is more concerned about his material things than his eternal home in heaven. But even more serious is the question of a Christian's spiritual motivations and goals. Christians are constantly trying to discover God's will for their lives, and yet the average Christian will openly admit that he does not really know God's will for his life. Because Christians are experiencing spiritual confusion, today's church, despite its numbers and its outward growth, probably is spiritually and morally weaker than it has ever been! We have bigger churches, better programs, more promotion, and more "decisions" than the church has known in its entire history. Yet, the average church of our day is desperately weak in "genuine," committed, Christian living. This weakness has so destroyed the powerful, spiritual impact of the church, that we have tended to substitute business for godliness. We have tried to convince ourselves that a congregation's size overrules carnality. Many of our preachers know how to promote, organize, and stimulate success, but they have never experienced the reality of genuine revival. Their own lives are desperately lacking in true godliness.

So desperate is the spiritual condition of today's church that not only is it necessary for the church to stand against worldliness from without, but from within as well! Many Christians have become totally lax concerning their spiritual responsibilities to God. Those responsibilities may touch any one of a number of given areas: personal devotional life, soul-winning, genuine Christian living, biblical standards of dress, appearance, and habits.

Some time ago, I was visiting in Chicago with a friend who took me to an expensive restaurant for dinner. Like all expensive restaurants, this one must have had a difficult time paying its light bill, and, therefore, it was rather dimly lit inside! I will never forget the comment of the waitress as she led us, virtually in total darkness, to a table. We were seated and handed a menu which no one could read. Then she commented, "If you will wait a few minutes, your eyes will become accustomed to the darkness, and you will be able to read the menu!" How true that same matter has become in relation to the twentieth century church! We have become so accustomed to the darkness of sin that it no longer appears to be darkness, but almost light. A new and flagrant outburst of sin will shock the general Christian public at first. Then, in time, they too will shift their moral and theological thinking to the point that they become "accustomed to the darkness."

The sad majority of Christians are more concerned about not becoming "too spiritual" rather than too worldly. Revival must begin in Christians, but it cannot come until one is willing to pay the price of revival in his own life. What is that price? It is the cost of sin. Until one comes to the place that he desires to obey God more than he is willing to disobey Him, he will not experience the cleansing empowerment of revival.

Do Christians Accept Responsibility?

One of the greatest essentials for genuine revival is a sense of personal responsibility on the part of every Christian. We are responsible for our personal relationship with God, we are responsible for the sin and the deceitfulness that we allow into our own lives, and we are responsible for failure to conform to the image of Christ. Today one often discovers a total sense of irresponsibility on the part of the average Christian toward his relationship with God. He spends little time in the study of the Bible and in prayer. His witnessing merely involves his inviting people to church, not to the Saviour.

If someone could computerize the amount of time during the last year that *you* actually spent in prayer would it be an embarrassment to you, or a cause of rejoicing? You see, we may claim that we want revival and that we want to see the power of God in our churches, but we are not willing to pay the price for that revival. Revival must not only begin in the house of God, it must begin with you! It must begin in your heart, and in your life, and in your relationship to the Saviour.

We have become indifferent to the will of God for our lives. Many times, we are devoted to building a "Christian empire," and are not committed to seeing a real and sincere moving of the Spirit of God in our own lives. All too often, what we accomplish by human means, we could accomplish without the power of the Spirit of God! The world around us is looking for sincerity of conviction within the church and within the lives of individual Christians. Until we have a personal concern and a sense of personal responsibility for revival, it will never happen. Pastor, until you begin to become personally concerned for revival in your heart, revival will never reach your church. Dear Christian, until you become personally concerned for revival in your life and in your family, it will never reach your community. Teenager, until you become concerned for revival in your life, or in your youth group, it will never happen in your school. When one has not experienced a genuine article, he will always be willing to accept a synthetic substitute. Perhaps the tragedy of this very hour is that so many Christians have been willing to accept the synthetic, and have never experienced the authentic, genuine power of the Spirit of God in their lives.

Does the Church Tolerate Sin?

Certainly the very place that one would not expect to find sin on the rampage would be in the church itself. But, unfortunately, this often is not the case. The Word of God reminds us that: ". . . Offenses must come, but woe to that man by whom the offense cometh!" (Matt. 18:7). What kind of sin is going on in your church right now? Many Christians who claim they are fighting the battle against sin and temptation are not even able to overcome the temptation to sin while sitting in a church service! Their thoughts wander on their own selfish, materialistic, and lustful desires. Often, our hearts are broken by hearing of the tragedy of sin and its effect in the lives of people who are actively involved in a church. What kind of sin is going on right now in your church? Though it is not promoted, it is being tolerated, Pastor, you are tolerating it! Toleration is the first step to compromise, which is the first step to failure.

For a moment be honest with yourself. Stop bragging to everyone about what a great church and grand attendance you have, and compile a list of sins being tolerated within your congregation. What are they: carnality, shallowness, bitterness, lying, cheating, adultery, divorce, fornication, covetousness, envy, deceit, gossip, pride, rebellion? Now read the list of reprobate sins in Romans 1!

Hebrews 12:15 reminds us, ". . . Look diligently . . . ; lest any root of bitterness springing up trouble you, and thereby many be defiled." In the Bible bitterness is stated to be a sin; and yet, more churches than not are torn by the problem of bitterness. Hard feelings exist between church members, between laymen and the pastor, between the pastor and his staff, and so forth. Bitterness is more communicable than the common cold. It spreads like a plague! Bitterness tolerated among genuine Christians will ruin and destroy the church faster than any other sin. Lying, cheating, stubbornness, rebellion: all of these serious sins are "tolerated" by some Christians and can destroy the moving of God among His people.

Is stubbornness that serious? Is rebellion that serious? First Samuel 12:53 states, "For rebellion is as the sin of witchcraft, and stubbornness is as iniquity and idolatry." Now if we are going to let God deal with sin from His point of view, we must call sin what God calls it. God says that stubbornness is as serious as idolatry. A person with a stubborn attitude worships the idol of self! Rebellion is as the sin of witchcraft in the sight of God. As we have seen a constant rise of rebellion among teenagers toward their parents, we also have seen a new and awakened interest in witchcraft, Satanism, and demon worship. The two always go hand in hand.

Undoubtedly, the greater responsibility in this area falls on the pastor. When God calls a man to lead his flock, part of that pastor's responsibility is to protect and guide his people. Pastor, God will hold you accountable for whether or not you have protected your people from wrong spiritual influences. As much as your heart is concerned, and often broken, over the failures of your people, realize that the heart of God is concerned and broken when you fail to give the clear direction that God would have you to give them. If sin is being tolerated in your church, much of the blame rests upon you. Therefore, revival must begin again in your heart. You must change your tolerant attitude toward the sins and offences of your people.

Do Christians Truly Love One Another?

The relationship shared by Jesus and his disciples

exemplifies the sanctified bond of friendship. Let it be said of you as it was said of them, ". . . ye also love one another." Jesus stated in John 13:35 that the only identifying mark set upon His people was the love they shared for each other. This love was their light to the unsaved world. Now we could set aside the principle of brotherly love among Christians and relegate it to the level of excessiveness; but if we do, we eliminate the one powerful quality or mark that God intended to use to set His people apart from the world. A popular song of our day says, "What the world needs now is love, sweet love." The world around us is desperately looking for someone that genuinely loves and cares for them. As David of old, they cry, "Does no man care for my soul?" (Ps. 142:4)

The absence of genuine love among Christians is one of the major hindrances to revival. Selfishness and jealousy among churches, pastors, and Christians have stopped the power of God from sweeping entire communities. The mark of distinction and power that rested upon the early church was the love of newborn Christians.

God chose love to convince an unsaved world that the message of Christ is true. Fundamentalists too long have reacted against an emphasis on love because of their desire to proclaim the truth. As the liberal theologians of the early twentieth century began to deny the truth and substitute it with an emphasis upon love as a means of salvation, the fundamentalists began to proclaim more vehemently the truth of the gospel which they so dearly loved. In so doing, however, we have too long proclaimed truth at the expense of love. An emphasis on genuine love for other Christians has come to mean "compromise" or "liberalizing." The truth of the Scripture is the only guideline that God gives us in regard to expressing truth and love together. The Word of God reminds us, ". . . speak the truth in love . . ." (Eph. 4:15). Both elements are necessary.

While the liberal has proclaimed love and eliminated the truth, the hyper-fundamentalist has proclaimed the truth at the expense of love. God's clear message to the genuine Christian is to proclaim the truth in love. We are to hold to fundamental, scriptural doctrine, to proclaim that doctrine, and to stand for that doctrine. Yet, we should do this, not out of bitterness and hatred, but out of love and devotion to the Saviour and concern for one another.

Genuine Christian love is the one unifying factor among God's people. Unity cannot be produced by ecumenical councils and movements. Genuine, spiritual unity among God's people can only be produced by the Spirit of God (Eph. 4:4). A genuine and deep sense of concern for the unsaved, as well as a constant compassion for believers, is evidence of God's working in the lives of His children. This evidence is essential for the outside world to believe what we claim to be when we take the name of Christ. A lack of love is an open expression of our spiritual weakness. Arguments among Christians, bitterness among church members, and rivalries that have often led to church splits, are not the sign of the working of the Spirit of God.

A lack of genuine Christian love among church members is the greatest deterent to genuine revival. This lack of love prevents unity in our search for the will and counsel of God. If there is a spirit of alienation or discord among Christians, they will not be able to come together or to allow the Holy Spirit to work in their lives. They will be unwilling to let

50   *Glory in the Church*

the Spirit of God examine their hearts to "see if there be any wicked way in me, and lead me in the way everlasting."

Ministers of the Word of God must stand for God's truth and proclaim those truths clearly and powerfully to the hearts of men. Their proclamation of that truth, however, must be done in an attitude of genuine love and concern so that the Spirit of God can draw the hearts of men to the Lord. God does not use one's personality, ability, or clever imagination to bring people to Himself. If we believe that, we are total Arminians in our thinking, our theology, and our practice. God has always chosen to use His Holy Spirit through His Word to bring people to the Saviour. If we bring people to ourselves, our personalities, our programs, or our systems, they will become merely names on "decision cards"—their names will not have been written down in the Lamb's book of life in heaven.

Can't a Pastor Have a "Specialized" Message?

It has always been a common error for preachers to "go off on a tangent." Often preaching may become autobiographical by revealing one's own inner struggles. Whenever the preacher of the gospel limits his message to a select area of truth, he is failing to proclaim the whole counsel of God (Acts 20:27). The Lord does not give his ministers the option of selecting one truth from the Bible and omitting another. If the gospel preacher does not present everything that is of benefit to his congregation (Acts 2:20), he cannot have a clear conscience before God and man.

Obstacles to Revival   51

Extremism in preaching always characterizes "splits" and factions. It stops the work of revival. Preachers are often reactionary in the declaration of their message. Some emphasize the truth at the expense of love; others so emphasize love that they eliminate the truth. Some promote only soul-winning; others, only the deeper life; others, the dispensations, . . . eschatology, . . . the distinctions of soteriology, . . . exposés of liberalism and communism, . . . the Bible and science, . . . the "gospel in the stars and pyramids," . . . numerology, . . . occultism . . . , and on the list could go.

It is obvious that every preacher will have his own areas of special interest. However, when these limited topics predominate his message, he is not really preaching the gospel. He is preaching his pet topic! The preaching of the gospel is the proclaiming of the good news of Christ: His death, burial, and resurrection. Genuine biblical preaching must be Christ-centered in its message.

Preaching the gospel means preaching Christ to the lost. It involves the proclamation of the person and work of Christ. The apostle Paul describes powerful preaching as being Christ-centered, expressing a warning against sin, teaching with all wisdom, and having the goal of presenting "every man perfect in Christ Jesus" (Col. 1:28-29).

What message do you have to proclaim to men? What message will stir their souls and be used by God to change their lives? It is none other than the preaching of Christ! While many other topics and areas of interest are helpful and applicable to both the saved and the lost, one must never omit the message of Christ. Throughout the history of the church, from Peter's message at Pentecost onward, it has been the message of Christ that has stirred revival.

Pastor, if you are not seeing genuine revival among your people, ask yourself, "What message am I preaching to them?" They can only respond to what you present. Decide right now to lay aside the spectacular and intellectual and call upon God to revive your heart with the message of Christ! May your messages be so filled with Him that they may be used by the Holy Spirit to bring your people genuine revival.

chapter 4

The Holy Spirit Gives Revival

"Oh Lord, revive thy work. . . ." (HABAKKUK 3:2)

The clear testimony of the Word of God explains that the work of revival is essentially the work of the Holy Spirit. "Not by works of righteousness which we have done, but according to His mercy He saved us, by the washing of regeneration, and renewing of the Holy Ghost" (Titus 3:5). The message of the gospel reaches out to a lost and desperate world. "But as many as received Him, to them gave He power to become the sons of God; even to them that believe on His name: which were born, not of blood, nor of the will of the flesh, nor of the will of man, but of God" (John 1:12-13). Salvation is entirely the work of God's grace in the behalf of man. No man can merit, earn, or even choose God's grace. ". . . God hath from the beginning chosen you to salvation through sanctification of the Spirit . . ." (1 Thess. 2:13). The experience of the new birth is a God-given experience to every believer. In Ezekiel 18:31 God promises a new heart and a new spirit for those who will stop their sinning.

The Scripture makes it clear that salvation is the work of the Holy Spirit, and that the renewing and reviving of God's church is also the work of the Spirit. Because of the emotional excesses of the Pentecostal movement early in this century, many fundamentalists have retreated from a strong emphasis upon the reality of the Holy Spirit. For every theological situation in which there is an overemphasis in one direction, there will always tend to be an overreaction in another direction. The overreaction is no more correct nor proper than the over-emphasis.

In order to appreciate the work of God properly, one must understand the true proportion of scriptural doctrine in every area. Dr. Sprague asks the question, "How do you account for the very powerful preaching of the apostles?" How did Peter touch the hearts of multitudes and convert so many of them? Why did the Philippian jailer remain indifferent until he became so anxious and alarmed that he finally trusted Jesus as his Saviour and Master and walked in His steps? And why was the ministry of the apostles so successful? Truly, there were strong prejudices against both them and the doctrine they preached. Yet, they undermined the pagan thrones and caused tens of thousands to gather around the standard of the Cross? The successes of the early Christians have been too hard for the jeering infidel to discount. There is no explanation except that a sovereign God works in the hearts of men by His Spirit, and that He dispenses His blessings whenever and wherever He chooses!

The Spirit Operates by Means of the Truth

God, in this sense, is called "the Spirit of truth," and men are also said to be "sanctified by the truth." The Holy Spirit uses the means of God's Word to change the hearts of men. The Scripture testifies that God's Word is truth (2 Cor. 6:7). In this great system of God's revealed truth, the Holy Spirit selects the spiritual stones to sling at the giants of sin and indifference.

The hour has come when we need to consider that God works in relation to the truth. He uses the truth of His Word to convince, convict, and convert the hearts of men. God does not use the overt exaggerations of prefabricated stories; He does not merely use "hot" illustrations, or the clever wit of men; He uses His truth. All though today's average sermon packs the cleverness of human wisdom, the propriety of pulpiteering, and a concern for man's condition, it often lacks genuine and substantial emphasis upon the truth of God's Word.

The great doctrines of the Bible are its truths. These must be emphasized and proclaimed in order for the Holy Spirit to move in genuine revival. In the parable of the sower we see that the Word of God, like a seed, must fall on fertile ground, an open heart (Matt. 13:23).

The Spirit Convinces Men of Sin

Jesus said of the Holy Spirit, "And when He is come, He will reprove the world of sin . . ." (John 16:8). The work of the Holy Spirit is convincing men of sin. On the day of Pentecost, the response to the message of Peter was, "Men and brethren, what shall we do?" The effect had been produced by the Holy Spirit. The Spirit of God convicts man of sin, and convinces him of his need of a Saviour. A person who is not convinced that he needs a Saviour will never come to that Saviour. A person who is not convinced of God's wrath will never see the need for finding One to save him from his sin. The response of the Philippian jailer: "Sirs, what must I do to be saved?" was not produced by casual efforts.

The working of God's Holy Spirit becomes evident when a person becomes convinced of his sin and is contrite (Acts 2:38). In this, the convinced sinner recognizes the difference between right and wrong. He comes to a genuine realization that sin has wrecked and ruined his life. He desires to be set free, not only from the penalty of sin, but from the misery of sin as well! Thus, conviction is accompanied by genuine remorse, repentance, and evidence of salvation (2 Cor. 7:10).

The preaching of God's standards for Christian living and the preaching of the Law is "the knowledge of sin." God's Law is nothing less than a transcript of His moral character, requiring all of His creatures to be holy as He is holy. God's law is the eternal standard of right, and every departure from it is sin. But if men are ignorant of this standard, they will, of course, be ignorant of their own sins. Only after the entire Law is presented to them, can men have any conviction of sin.

God's laws are learned from the Scripture, the Word of God. And, it is through His word that man learns the Christian way. The intensity and the volume of voice that the preacher produces will not bring true conviction. The Word of God, alone, brings conviction to the heart of the sinner. Undoubtedly, the clearest reason why we lack a genuine conviction of sin among evangelical Christians today, and the greatest reason why we are not now experiencing revival on a nationwide scale, is because the average Christian is not "convinced" of sin. We have become "too accustomed to the darkness." Many who profess to be Christians have made every attempt to rationalize and excuse away their sin.

Some have tried to lie about their sin, even as Ananias and Sapphira. Others have attempted to cover their sin as Achan did. Many condemn others for their sin, even though the Scripture reminds them that ". . . for wherein thou judgest another, thou condemnest thyself" (Rom. 2:1). People tend to condemn in others the very things of which they themselves are guilty. Condemnation of others is a psychological symptom of a guilty conscience. When Adam and Eve were confronted with their sin, Adam immediately attempted to blame Eve and God for the problem. "It is the woman Thou hast given me." Blaming others for our own problems and condemning wrong in the lives of others is one of the great weaknesses of today's church. Jesus said, "Thou hypocrite, first cast out the beam out of thine own eye; and then shalt thou see clearly to cast out the mote out of thy brother's eye" (Matt. 7:5).

The favorite twentieth century method of rationalizing sin is to rename it, or call it something other than what it is. This is the age of the euphemism. Sin is called moral weakness; rebellion has become "abnormal social development;" murder is blamed on mental illness. Christian, you may lie about your sin, but it will not go away! You may try to cover your sin or blame someone else for it. You may attempt to justify your sin but you still will have no victory over it. Revival begins when Christians let the Holy Spirit deal with sin in their lives.

The Spirit Produces Conversion

Genuine conversion is the turning of the soul from sin to holiness. Jesus said, ". . . Except a man be born of water and of the Spirit, he cannot enter into the kingdom of God" (John 3:5). The work which the Holy Spirit performs is the total renovation of man's nature. The Holy Spirit transforms an enemy of God into a friend. Whereas, we were once at enmity with God, we are now the recipients of His blessing. The work of the Holy Spirit is preparation for conversion. Over one hundred and fifty years ago, Dr. Sprague had insights that we need today as never before. He states, "The Spirit, in His converting influences, instead of bringing the truth to bear directly upon the conscience, addresses it to the world and the affections." In genuine conversion the Spirit of God begins to move upon the will of man, which is bent against God and is in bondage to sin. The apostle Paul said, "There is none that understandeth, there is none that seeketh after God" (Rom. 3:11). Genuine conversion is so totally transforming that the natural man who once possessed "a heart of stone" is now given "a new heart" (Ezek. 11:19). The man, who previously had loved and chosen sin, experiences such a dynamic change that he chooses love and holiness.

The work of conversion involves a different emphasis than the work of conviction. Because of the incorruptible seed, the Word of God, men are born to newness of life. But, it is by the gospel that this work is effective. It is the Law that made the sinner tremble, but it is the gospel that brings peace and gladness to his soul. It is the Law that caused the three thousand to be convicted in heart; it is the gospel—the crucified and living Saviour—that melted them into contrition and transformed them into disciples. The Law anticipates the eternal wrath of God; the gospel proclaims the good news of hope to the helpless sinner. It is the gospel that assures the sinner of eternal life and forgiveness of sin through Christ's atoning blood. The sinner, through the agency of the Holy Spirit, seizes this truth, melts down in humble submission at the cross, and discovers life rather than death.

The Spirit Develops Holiness

The apostle Paul stated, "We are bound to thank God always for you, brethren, as it is meet, because that your faith groweth exceedingly, and the charity of every one of you all toward each other aboundeth" (2 Thess. 2:3). The act of regeneration leaves the soul far from the state of perfect holiness. Though man is given sanctification at the time of salvation, he really begins a lifelong struggle with sin and self. Thus, there is much done subsequent to regeneration to prepare us for heaven. The Holy Spirit now begins to operate on every aspect of the soul; the conscience, the will, and the emotions. The whole spiritual man is brought into the design of God's eternal purpose by His power. And, every part of the Law and the gospel are used by this Divine Agent in carrying forward His sanctifying work. "All Scripture is given by inspiration of God . . ." (2 Tim. 3:16).

In every revival we distinctly recognize the sovereignty of God. Whether in the salvation of one soul, or in the conversion of hundreds, it is clear that God moves by His sovereign choice. Thus, the Word of God states, "The wind bloweth where it listeth, and thou hearest the sound thereof, but canst not tell whence it cometh, or whither it goeth: so is every one that is born of the Spirit" (John 3:8). And so too, is every genuine revival of religion! Man cannot control the Spirit of God. God moves in power wherever He chooses to move. The preaching of the same messages in one church, or in one community, may bring different results. Some may reject the message, while others with similar background and similar preparation, accept the Spirit of God and blessings never before comprehended by the heart of man.

As the Spirit of God begins to operate in the lives of men, the audience itself sends a message to the careless sinner. As people listen intently to God's Word, their faces carry a message to those around them. The room in which they sit can become so changed that the disobedient sinner can sense the Spirit of God at work. Naturally, this will open his ears to God's truth, so that the solemnity of conviction may take the place of sympathy and begin to draw his heart to Christ.

The Spirit Uses the Example of True Christians

There can be no doubt that every reborn Christian is either a steppingstone to heaven or a stumbling block over which the lost plunge into hell. God uses the lives of His people as "epistles known and read of every man" to move the hearts of the unsaved. Often, nothing will speak more convincingly to the heart of the indifferent unbeliever than the genuine response of God's people. It is not unusual for the most violent and worldly people to break under genuine conviction when they see God convicting, moving, and stirring the hearts of His people. In our revival crusades we have seen unbelievers converted when God's people respond to the clear directions of the Word of God allow their hearts to be broken and moved by the power of God's truth. However, when God's people resist obedience to the clear truth of the Word of God, the unsaved will also resist the power of the Saviour.

The world is looking for genuineness and reality in the lives of those who claim to know Christ. The message of the Word of God demands that the Christian seek a new level of obedience in relation to confession of sin, concern for one's family, clearing one's conscience, seeking forgiveness for bitternesses, the exercise of serving faith, and any one of a number of spiritual areas. When God's people respond in obedience of the Word of God, the Holy Spirit uses their example to convict and then bring others who are lost to the point of conversion. Certainly the conviction that Saul of Tarsus "kicked against" was the true godliness he saw in the lives of the Christians, like Stephen, whom he persecuted.

Recognizing the necessity of genuine Spirit-controlled, Spirit-directed revival, we must labor with a sense of dependence upon God. All our efforts to plan and program will come to no avail if the Holy Spirit is not actively and powerfully moving upon lives. A spirit of dependence upon God withdraws attention and credit from men and brings honor to the Lord. Much of what is called "contemporary evangelism" is nothing more than a personality evangelism of preachers who are drawing attention to themselves, their personalities, and their programs. Thus, "they have their reward." Genuine preaching is so Christ-centered that it brings the attention and the credit to Christ alone. Whenever Christ's people are truly humbled before Him, whenever they deeply feel their own emptiness, whenever they are willing to be used as mere instruments in the hand of Almighty God, then you will find the outpouring of God's richest blessings. God is a jealous God. He will not share His glory with any man. Revival is not the result of some evangelist's clever statements, or invitation methods; it is not the result of pizza nights, "youth nights," and "junior nights." It is the result of God moving on the lives of those in need of His blessing. Revival has always come by the power of God, it will always come by the power of God, and it will come only by the power of God!

chapter 5

Prayer: The Power of Revival

"Sow to yourselves in righteousness, reap in mercy; break up your fallow ground: for it is time to seek the Lord, till he come and rain righteousness upon you."   (HOSEA 10:12)

While it is true that revival comes through God's grace and the working of the Holy Spirit, it is also true that every great revival has come as a result of daily prayer by men of God. During the famous Welsh Revival (1904-05) more than 100,00 people were converted within five months. Evan Roberts, used so greatly of God during that revival, had prayed for revival daily for thirteen years! William McColloch, the pastor at Cambuslang, Scotland, prayed continually for revival for over a year before God burst upon his congregation in February, 1742.

While the men God used in revival labored much, studied much, and preached much, they also prayed much. "They were much alone with God," declares Dr. Bonar, "replenishing their own souls out of the living fountain that out of them might flow to their people rivers of living water." Often those who are sincerely seeking to win souls and feed believers exhaust their energies on external duties such as preaching, visiting, and counseling, and overlook the absolute necessity of enriching and elevating their own souls through prayer and fasting.

Break Up Your Fallow Ground

The prophet Hosea preached a revival message to Israel even though he lived during the nation's darkest hour. He pleaded with the people: "Sow to yourselves in righetousness, reap in mercy; break up your fallow ground . . ." (Hos. 10:12). What is "fallow ground?" It is unused or unplowed ground. For many Christians, their "fallow ground" is their prayer life. Too many prayers represent little more than a repetitious Protestant "rosary" (minus the beads)!

The time has come to break up our fallow prayer ground and seek the Lord. The unused resources of prayer available to every Christian are almost staggering. The Scripture says that Elijah "prayed earnestly," and God changed the environment of a nation. ". . . The effectual fervent prayer of a righteous man availeth much" (Js. 5:16). Twentieth century Christianity stands in need of effective prayer.

Can a nation actually be changed by the prayers of a few? Yes! John Knox prayed: "Give me Scotland, else I die!" Evan Roberts persisted in prayer for Wales, John Wesley became broken over England. Jeremiah Lanphier besought God for months for revival in America in 1857. In each case God answered their prayers.

An excellent scriptural example is Daniel. Having lived nearly seventy years through the Babylonian Captivity, the elderly Daniel was reminded, after reading the prophet Jeremiah, that the captivity of

Israel would last for only seventy years (605-536 B.C.). The shocking reminder made him realize that their captivity was nearly over, and Israel would soon return to their own land. It was then 538 B.C., the year that Belshazzar would be slain, and the Persians would take the kingdom. Daniel, realizing that the people of Israel had grown accustomed to the pomp of Babylon, knew that his people were not spiritually ready to return home.

In Daniel 9:3-19, we read the old prophet's prayer of confession on behalf of the people of Israel: "We have sinned, and have committed iniquity, and have done wickedly, and have rebelled . . ." (Dan. 9:5). He went on to acknowledge that all of Israel's troubles were the result of the "curse of the law," had brought on by their disobedience (v. 13). He made his confession before God: "confessing my sin and the sin of my people Israel" (v. 20). Then God sent Gabriel with a message of encouragement to Daniel.

A few weeks after this prayer, the Babylonian Empire fell and was replaced by Persia. By the spring of 536 B.C., Cyrus the Persian would decree the end of Israel's captivity and their return to the land of their fathers. Can the prayer of one man, or a few, change the course of an entire nation? Both Scripture and church history indicate that it can! America and English-speaking peoples in general have not seen revival in the twentieth century because no one has persisted in prayer for it! The time has come to unite in prayer for revival: "God give us America, before it is too late!"

The Expectation of Faith

Prayer involves three major facets: preparation,

supplication, and expectation. The Scripture tells us why we often do not get our prayers answered. The reason has to do with the preparation of our hearts.

1. *Preparation:* Obedience is always a prerequisite to blessing (1 Sam. 15:22). However, one may obtain genuine obedience through genuine self-examination in light of the objective truth of the Scripture. God will never send the blessings of His Spirit where there is unconfessed sin. "If I regard iniquity in my heart, the Lord will not hear me" (Ps. 66:18). "Regarding" sin means having a favorable attitude toward sin, or a desire to "hold on to" that sin.

Confession and obedience is always necessary before you can come to the throne of grace and gain your request. The brief list below may well indicate why you have not gained your request from God. God will not answer your prayers if you:

Regard sin (Ps. 66:18).
Seek material things (Jas. 4:3).
Hold bitterness (Mark 11:25).
Return evil for good (Prov. 17:13).
Fail to minister to your family (1 Pet. 3:7).

2. *Supplication:* If revival is really nothing more than a "new beginning of obedience to God" (Finney), then it cannot come with mere promotion alone. Revival must come with deep humility and repentance even among God's people. The proper spiritual preparation readies us for a deeper and more meaningful expression of supplication.

The prayer meeting on the day of Pentecost is simply described: "These all continued with one accord in prayer and supplication . . ." (Acts 1:14). Notice the essential elements of this prayer. There is nothing spasmodic or intermittent about it. On the contrary, the pentecostal prayer meeting was characterized by constancy, fervor, and unity. Powerful results do not come from impotent prayers. Powerful praying is not done with a glorified and amplified "Now I lay me down to sleep." True prayer involves fasting, discipline, and persistence. When Jesus' disciples, unable to deal with a demon-possessed boy, saw Jesus transform him, they asked: "Why couldn't we help the child?" The Saviour replied: ". . . This kind can come forth by nothing, but by prayer and fasting" (Mark 9:29).

3. *Expectation:* Everywhere in the Scripture prayer is linked to faith, especially in the messages of Jesus. ". . . Thy faith hath made thee whole" (Mark 5:34); ". . . according to your faith be it unto you" (Matt. 9:29); ". . . if ye have faith, . . . ye shall not only do this . . . and all things, whatsoever ye shall ask in prayer, believing, ye shall receive" (Matt. 21:21-22); ". . . have faith in God . . . what things soever ye desire, when we pray, believe that ye receive them, and ye shall have them" (Mark 11:22-24).

One cannot believe something without genuinely expecting it. "Faith" and "hope" are scriptural terms for "confident expectation." Real faith believes and receives. "But as many as *received* him, to them gave he power to become sons of God, even to them that *believe* on his name" (John 1:12). Expectation and determination in prayer are essential to revival. Boldness or determination is necessary to be successful in prayer. Bonar said: "Timidity shuts many a door of usefulness, and loses many a precious opportunity; it wins no friends, while it strengthens every enemy. Nothing is lost by boldness, nor gained by fear."

Begin to pray and work with the effort of determination and the diplomacy of patience. "For it is God which worketh in you both to will and to do of his good pleasure" (Phil. 2:13). God will work in

His sovereign time, but He will work! Do not be afraid of a lack of faith. Rather, be bold and expect great things." Too long people have feared to ask God for revival in America. The time has now come that thousands are seeking and ready to believe the renewing Power of God.

Pray With Spirit and Understanding

The apostle Paul was a man of constant prayer. Not only do his epistles reveal this, but the story of the conversion of the Philippian jailer in Acts 16, illustrates that Paul's prayers were answered. In 1 Corinthians 14, Paul is dealing with the confusion that had arisen over tongues. "For if the trumpet give an uncertain sound," he proclaims, "who shall prepare himself to the battle? So likewise ye, except ye utter by the tongue words *easy to be understood,* how shall it be known what is spoken? for ye shall speak into the air?" (1 Cor. 8-9). Not only should our messages be simple and understandable, but also our prayers.

In verse fifteen, Paul states: "What is it then? I will pray with the spirit, and I will pray with the understanding also. . . ." The implication is that praying "in the spirit" need not be unintelligible, but ought to express a simple truth. This is the kind of prayer we need; prayer that finds clear access to the throne of grace and gets results! It is powerful yet simple.

If every messenger of the Word of God bathed his sermon in spiritual prayer, heaven would move his listeners beyond his own expectations. If we spent as much time in prayer as we do in study, our Sunday services would shine with the glory of God as did the face of Moses. The result would be "glory in the church." Were every message set aflame from heaven, there would be fewer complaints from our listeners. Whatever might be lost in elaborate expression or exactness of style, would be more than compensated for by a "double portion of the Spirit." A sermon that calls attention to the messenger and does not reflect the glory of God has not been prepared in prayer.

A heart-rending, agonizing perparation of prayer will cause your words to glow with the glory of heaven and to touch the heart of saint and sinner alike. The goal of this kind of prayer-preaching is people. It is no mere oration, lecture, or devotional. This preaching bears the stamp of heaven. It is doctrinal, but it is not "dead orthodoxy." The awesome doctrines of the Word of God touch men's souls causing them to cry: "Abba, Father."

Thomas Shepard of Cambridge so prepared each sermon with prayer that it was said of him: "He scarcely ever preached a sermon but some or other of his congregation were struck with great distress, and cried out in agony, 'What shall I do to be saved?'" In recounting his early ministry, Charles Spurgeon remarked: "There is scarcely a sermon here that is not marked with the conversion of a soul!" Learn to pray in the spirit and you will preach with power.

Prayer and Fasting

During the twentieth century, fasting has become the most neglected spiritual exercise of all. Many simply ignore it as excessive or unessential for our age. However, this was not the testimony of the early church. There are seventy-four references to fasting in the Bible, of which twenty-nine appear in the New Testament. Of these, there are ten references to the diciples' fasting and nine statements of fasting being practiced by the early church.

Notice that the church at Antioch "fasted and prayed" before commissioning Barnabas and Paul (Acts 13:3). When they won several converts on the first missionary journey, they too "prayed with fasting" (Acts 14:23) before ordaining elders in every church they had established. Paul refers to his own fasting and then enjoins the church to join him in 2 Corinthians 6:5. Every reference to fasting in Scripture is seen in a positive and important light (except the contentious and self-righteous fasting of the Pharisees).

The spiritual foundation of genuine fasting was laid sufficiently in the Old Testament: ". . . I humbled my soul with fasting . . ." (Psalm 35:13); "So we fasted and besought our God . . ." (Ezra 8:23). Daniel sought greater understanding from Scripture "by prayer and with fasting" (Dan. 9:3). National fasts were often proclaimed in Israel (see 2 Chron. 20:3; Ezra 8:21; Joel 1:14).

The function of fasting is simply not eating solid food (Mark 8:3). The purpose of fasting brings victory over sin and temptation. Fasting is the spiritual discipline where one learns to feed his soul while denying his physical nature. In Isaiah 58, we read the phophet's description of the wrong, self-righteous use of fasting: ". . . Ye fast for strife and debate" (v. 4). The prophet goes on to declare that God has not chosen fasting to add yet another burden to men's souls, but relieve such burdens. "Is not this the fast that I have chosen? to loose the bands of wickedness, to undo the heavy burdens, and to let the oppressed go free, and that ye break every yoke?" (v. 6).

Biblical prayer and fasting is the "catharsis" of God for the souls of saints. Isaiah goes on to say: "Then shall thy light break forth as the morning, and thine health shall spring forth speedily; and thy righteousness shall go before thee; the *glory of the Lord* shall be thy reward. Then shalt thou call, and the Lord shall answer; thou shalt cry, and he shall say, Here I am" (vv. 8-9). This is "glory in the church!"

Prayer with fasting involves both discipline and self-denial. Paul declared in 1 Corinthians 9:27 that he beat his body and kept it under subjection. It is now time for concerned Christians to genuinely seek the face of God for revival in our land. We need a time of real national prayer and fasting. God has the solution: "and I . . . will heal their land" (2 Chron. 7:14). One day in eternity his national healing touch will be felt by all the saved: "In the midst of . . . it (the new heaven) . . . on either side of the river was . . . the tree of life . . . and the leaves of the tree were for the healing of the nations" (Rev. 22:2). Oh, that we might experience a touch of that spiritual healing even now!

chapter 6

Neglected Doctrines of Revival: Repentance and the Lordship of Christ

"They that dwell under his shadow shall return; they shall revive as the corn, and grow as the vine: . . . Ephraim shall say, What have I to do any more with idols? I have heard him, and I observed him . . ."
(HOSEA 14:7-8)

When genuine revival comes with heaven-sent power, individual lives are transformed. When we hear from heaven and catch a fresh glimpse of the glory of Christ, we have no desire to "return to idols." The power of revival always brings change: changed lives, changed churches, and changed communities. In every great revival during the history of the church, there were sweeping affects on a large number of people.

The powerful transformation brought by revival does not happen accidentally. It is the result of the convicting ministry of the Holy Spirit through the distinctive doctrines of the revival preachers. There is depth and power in this type of preaching. The trumpet may give no "uncertain sound" to either saint or sinner. Revival preaching must be masculine and fearless, falling on the audience with tremendous

73

power. It need not be vehement or violent, but it must be solemn and weighty, piercing sharper than a two-edged sword. The revival preacher is a most delicate surgeon, not a hacking butcher. It is time to reach into the Shepherd's pouch of Scripture and select a stone that will fell the giant of sin!

Serious spiritual conviction will not result from doctrines lightly preached. The full significance of scriptural truth must be brought to bear on every subject. During the twentieth century, American Christianity has not lacked preachers who have strongly upheld the essential fundamental doctrines: the inspiration of Scripture, the deity of Christ, His virgin birth, His vicarious atonement for sin, and His literal second coming.

Each of these doctrines is an absolute "fundamental" to real biblical Christianity. They have been proclaimed strongly by great men of God in this generation. Still, there have been only rare outbursts of genuine revival. This is not to say that there have been none, for there have been those singular "divine moments" when God has moved.

This leads us to ask, "Why not more?" One may offer many human suggestions without coming to the real answer. For example, Finney, after he sensed that the flame of revival had died out, tried to implement the "mechanics" of revival (confession and immediate decision) without success. Today many churches and evangelists have people parading down the aisle, but these converts lack a real sense of conviction for sin. Finney had the mechanics but no results; some, today, have seeming "results" with no real spiritual response.

Rationalizations for why this has happened could become endless. Let me suggest a far more serious reason: doctrine! While maintaining the essential "fundamentals," many fundamentalists have added nonessentials to their list of absolutes. The "truth-only" crowd has added more "truth" and, therefore, more reasons for "separation." The "love-only" group has added more "love" and, therefore, more incentive for "inclusion." Both have often missed the two key revival doctrines: repentance and the Lordship of Christ.

The Doctrine of Repentance

What is the "neglected doctrine" of the twentieth century? Repentance! Begin to preach it and revival will burst forth. In *every* great revival era there was always a strong emphasis on repentance. When revival dies out, so does strong preaching on repentance. The clearest evidence that we have not had nationwide revival in our lifetime is the absence of preaching the doctrine of repentance.

At the turn of the century, James Burns wrote the book *Revivals: Their Laws and Leaders.* In the opening chapter he discusses the "laws" of revival, as well as the "laws" of the absence of revival. "The first tendency," he writes, "Is for the doctrine of the church to lose its power of convicting the conscience, convincing the mind, or moving the heart." He goes on to point out that spiritual decay brings with it a formality of worship in which the "ritual" is so exalted that it crushs the spirit.

Revival breaks open all spiritual tombs. Revival comes with sweeping ethical change because of the preaching of repentance. It leaves behind joyful and changed lives. When the first breath of revival touches the heart of the church, men instantly spring up as if awakening from some deep trance. They break the chains of lethargy, wash off the odor of spiritual deadness, and joyfully return to simplicity of worship and sincerity of life.

What Does Repentance Involve?

There are two basic usages of the term "repent" (or "repentance") in the Scripture. The Hebrew word *nacham* means to "be penitent" or "sorry" (for example, ". . . it repented the Lord that he had made man . . .", Gen. 6:6). However, the word *shub* means "to turn back" (for example ". . . repent, and turn from idols . . .", Ezek. 14:6). This latter usage implies a definite response of change. Likewise, the Greek of the New Testament has two such usages. *Metamelomai* means "to be concerned" or "sorry" (for example, ". . . Judas . . . repented himself . . .", Matt. 27:3). On the other hand, the word *metanoeo* means "to have another mind" or "to change one's mind" (for example, ". . . repent ye therefore, and be converted . . .", Acts 3:19). It is this latter usage that concerns us in the doctrine of repentance.

A change of mind evidences itself in a change of action. Some have strongly argued, however, that "repentance" is only a change of mind and does not involve a change of action, which they contend would be a "work." Since man is not saved by works, they reason that it is not necessary to repent in order to be saved. The advocates of this view point out that the New Testament calls upon the sinner to "believe" no less than 115 times, making no mention at all to repentance.

76   *Glory in the Church*

They then conclude that faith is the only condition of salvation and that repentance is not required of anyone at all, or required only of the Jews, or, finally, required only of Christians *after* they are saved.

Is Repentance a Condition of Salvation?

The absence of a doctrinal statement in one part of the Scripture in no way negates its emphasis in other parts. If there is substantial evidence of the requirement of repentance in the Scripture, then it does not matter whether it is mentioned in connection with "believe" 115 times. Obviously, it is assumed. Let's examine the evidence.

1. *The Message of Jesus:* Jesus preached repentance as a condition to salvation no less than nineteen times. In addition, He called the church to repent seven times in the book of Revelation! All three Synoptic Gospels record His own statement of His earthly ministry: ". . . I am not come to call the righteous, but sinners to repentance" (Matt. 9:13; Mark 2:17; Luke 5:32). The only way to escape repentance as an obvious "condition" to salvation is to fall back on the erroneous idea that He preached this only to Jewish sinners!

Jesus' initial preaching centered around the theme of repentance: ". . . Repent ye: for the kingdom of heaven is at hand" (Matt: 3:2, 4:17). National repentance was the condition under which Israel was to receive the Kingdom which, of course, they rejected. In Luke 13:3, Jesus strongly announced, ". . . Except ye repent, ye shall all likewise perish." In the parable of the "lost sheep" Jesus declared, "I say unto you, that likewise joy shall be in heaven over one sinner that repenteth" (Luke 15:7). Did He believe that sinners needed to repent in order to gain heaven? The answer is obvious. It is also true that believers can repent and often need to do so. Yet, their need for repentance in no way proves that the message of repentance is only for them.

2. *The Message of Peter and Paul:* Examine now the message and ministry of the apostles. In Luke's version of the "great commission" he records Jesus' direction to His disciples: ". . . that repentance and remission of sins should be preached in His name among all nations, beginning at Jesusalem" (Luke 24:47). Is the message of repentance for the Jews only? Obviously not! It is to be preached to all nations. Did the disciples obey this command?

Peter and Paul are the two major sources of New Testament preaching on repentance. In Acts 2:38, Peter urged the unconverted Jews and proselytes at the Feast of Pentecost to "repent and be baptised." In his second sermon at the beautiful gate of the Temple, he thundered: "Repent ye therefore, and be converted, that your sins may be blotted out . . ." (Acts 3:19). Years later in 2 Peter 3:9 he wrote: "The Lord . . . is long-suffering to us-ward, not willing that any should perish, but that all should come to repentance." Again, it is clear in this context that if one does not repent, he will perish.

Paul also both preached repentance and wrote about it. Addressing the Greek "pagans" on Mars Hill in Athens he said: "God . . . now commandeth all men every where to repent . . ." (Acts 17:30). As far as the text indicates, there were no Jews present. In Acts 20, Paul, having concluded his third missionary journey, was sailing home to Antioch and stopped off at Miletus on the coast of Asia Minor.

There he sent a message to the elders of the beloved church at Ephesus to come for a final meeting with him. At that time he reviewed everything he felt was essential in reminding them of ". . . all the counsel of God" (v. 27).

In his farewell message, Paul clearly states: ". . . I kept back nothing that was profitable unto you, but have showed you, and have taught you publicly, and from house to house, testifying both to the Jews, and also to the Greeks, repentance toward God, and faith toward our Lord Jesus Christ (Acts 20:20-21). It is quite clear in this message that the repentance Paul had taught them was part of that essential counsel of God. Again, this passage makes it clear that both Jews and Gentiles are to repent. It also clearly states that repentance preceeds faith (as does Acts 3:19, 11:18; 2 Cor. 7:9-10; Luke 24:47; and 2 Tim. 2:25).

Even though the injunction to "believe" or exercise "faith" appears over one hundred times alone, this fact does not prove that repentance is not a condition to salvation. Such an argument is an argument based upon silence in that it is merely an assumption and not a proven fact. Wherever one finds both faith and repentance *together* in the same passage, he will observe the same formula; repentance *always* preceeds faith, understanding, or conversion!

Dr. Ironside's observation on Acts 20:21, is worth noting. He points out that the statement, ". . . *repentance* toward God, and *faith* toward our Lord Jesus Christ," suggests that repentance involves a change of one's attitude toward God the Father. It is this change that prepares one for the response of faith toward Christ. He cites the case of the Philippian jailer, who had already fallen down under conviction and cried: "Sirs, what must I do to be saved?" The jailer did not need to be told to repent, since he was already giving outward evidence of repentance. To him the message of the gospel was: ". . . Believe on the Lord Jesus Christ, and thou shalt be saved . . ." (Acts 16:31). Yet, only one chapter later in Acts 17:29, Paul, now preaching to unrepentant intellectuals, says: "God . . . now commandeth all men every where to repent!" Why the change? These intellectuals could not genuinely believe in Christ until they first changed their basic attitude toward God and His Word.

This is the reason for the failure of so much modern evangelism. Too many preachers are asking unrepentant sinners to "believe", and they cannot possibly believe because of their hardened sinful hearts. Thus, "professions" are made which are not genuine. False assurance causes these unrepentant "church members" to appear to be so-called "carnal Christians," when in fact they have never been born again.

3. *Is this Evidence from Acts merely "Transitional"?* There is only one real argument left to those who deny that repentance is to be preached to saved and unsaved alike. It is the "hyper-dispensational" idea that everything in the book of Acts is transitional from the Old Covenant, and therefore does not apply to us today.

While it is true that certain concepts in the book of Acts represent a definitely "transitional stage" (for example, the continued preaching of the kingdom in the early chapters of Acts, miracles done by the apostles, attending synagogue Sabbath services, and keeping certain Jewish feasts), this does not relegate the entire book into the Old Testament era. One major fact needs to be remembered: the book of Acts is the first chapter of church history. While the Epistles tell us what the church IS, Acts tells us what it DID!

It should also be remembered that the book of Acts was actually written *after* many of the epistles. Now, while it contains a record of the early days of the church, it also continues up to the time of Paul's (first?) imprisonment at Rome. For example, when Paul stands before King Agrippa in Acts 26, most of his earthly life has already passed. And yet, even at this late date he declares: "Whereupon, O King Agrippa, I was not disobedient unto the heavenly vision: but showed first unto them of Damascus, and at Jerusalem, and throughout all the coasts of Judea, and then to the *Gentiles,* that they should *repent* and turn to God, and do works meet for repentance" (vv. 19-20).

Three times in his epistles, Paul refers to repentance: Romans 2:4; 2 Corinthians 7:9-10; 2 Timothy 2:25 (the last letter he ever wrote)! The excuse that the evidence from Acts is merely "transitional" is fallacious! In 2 Corinthians 7, Paul warmheartedly says: "Now I rejoice, not that ye were made sorry, but that ye sorrowed to repentance . . . for godly sorrow worketh repentance to salvation . . ." (vv. 9:10). Man must repent and believe the gospel to be saved.

4. *Is Repentance a "Work"?* One of the major arguments of those who reject the doctrine of repentance as a condition of salvation is the contention that this makes repentance a "work." To which the obvious reply is that repentance is no more a "work" than is faith!

Remember that repentance *(metanoeo)* is a "change of mind" that leads to a change of action. Some deny this, saying that it is only a change of mind (to do this, they must totally sidestep Acts 26:20, ". . . Repent and turn to God, and do works meet for repentance"). Repentance, in the Scripture, clearly comes before "turning to God" in trust or faith. The "works" of repentance then follow the turn to God in faith. Thus:

REPENTANCE	FAITH	FRUIT
(mind changed toward God)	(total trusting of the finished work of Christ)	("works giving evidence that the repentance and faith were genuine).

We need to remember clearly that God asks no man to change his own life, for no man can. He does not ask man either to repent or to believe by means of his own ability. Faith, if it originated from some inherent quality within man, would be just as much a "work" as repentance. The Greek text of the Scripture makes it clear that we are saved on the *basis* of grace (not on the basis of our "having faith"). Man is saved on the basis of God's grace, but through the instrumental means of faith. Therefore, even faith is not a "work" since it, like repentance, is a gift of God.

That repentance is God-given and does not originate from within man, is clearly stated in the three passages on repentance that we have yet to consider: Acts 11:18, ". . . They . . . glorified God, saying, Then hath God also to the Gentiles *granted repentance* unto life"; Romans 2:4, ". . . not knowing that the goodness of God *leadeth thee to repentance*"; 2 Timothy 2:25, ". . . if God peradventure *will give them repentance* to the acknowledging of the truth. . . ." Where does repentance originate? It comes from God. Nevertheless, God holds man responsible for his individual actions and calls on him to "repent and be converted." While the sovereignty of God's operations are not limited by the devices of men, His message is still to be boldly proclaimed to all!

Repentance is not a work, but it is the solemn necessity of a proper response to the gospel. If a man is engaged to be married to a certain woman, then it is fair to say that they are headed toward the goal of marriage, even if they are standing still. If he changes his mind and ultimately breaks the engagement, they are no longer headed toward the goal of marriage. He has not necessarily moved out of town or left the area; but his change of mind has led to a change in his course of action. When did his direction toward the original goal change? Not when he actually broke the engagement, but when he definitely changed his mind about the girl. You see, it is virtually impossible to have a change of mind without automatically and concurrently having a change of action.

Lordship of Christ

The contemporary weakness in the concept of biblical repentance has led to a total misunderstanding of the Lordship of Christ. If a person must genuinely repent in order to be saved (as scriptural evidence clearly indicates), then this act necessarily involves an absolute and unconditional surrender to Christ. The very same people who deny the doctrine of repentance also reject the idea that one "surrenders" at the point of salvation.

Contemporary fundamentalism has almost been

totally duped by this latter idea. Hundreds of preachers wrongly divide the person and work of Christ between His Saviorhood and His Lordship. They assert that men need to receive Jesus as Savior and, at a later time, make Him Lord of their lives. This idea is nothing more than a "sub-holy" and "quasi-second blessing" idea! It is one step above pentecostalism.

1. *No Scriptural Evidence for "Secondary" Lordship:* Nowhere does the inspired Word of God "divide" the person of Christ. The Scripture presents a whole Christ to meet the entire needs of the whole man. The sinner is not saved in "stages." He is transformed by the experience of the new birth produced by our Lord and Saviour Jesus Christ.

You will not find one verse of Scripture asking you to make Christ "Lord of your life" subsequent to salvation! Yet, many fundamentalists ask their listeners to do this constantly. While it is certainly true that every believer "grows in grace" and in the sanctifying processes of the Holy Spirit, it is still true that at the point of salvation Christ is "Lord" of the believer's life. In addition, it is not true that He ceases to be Lord at any subsequent time in the Christian's life.

Christ is *always* Lord, and the believer is *always* His servant. The question of spirituality is not whether one will "still allow Christ to be his Lord," but whether he will obey or disobey the One who will always be his Lord. The Christian may be an obedient or disobedient servant, but he is still a servant, "earmarked" for all eternity. Christ never ceases to be his Lord no matter how disobedient he becomes, and there is not the first verse of Scripture that even implies this! Let us examine the biblical terms for "lord" and "servant:".

a) "Master" (teacher)—*didaskalos:* this term is

Glory in the Church

used for Jesus forty-five times, and though it is translated "master" in the King James Version, it means "teacher."

b) "Master" (teacher)—*rabbi:* this word is used eight times for Jesus; this term also means basically "teacher."

c) "Master" (lord)—*kurios:* this word is usually translated "lord" (see below); the King James Version, however, uses it twice as "master" in referring to Jesus ("your master in heaven...", Eph. 6:9; Col. 4:1). It is also used in the statement: "No man can serve two masters..." (Matt. 6:24; Luke 16:13).

The term "Lord" in the Old Testament has a different meaning from that found in the New Testament. "Lord" is used in the Old Testament to translate *adon* (master or owner); *adonai* (Lord God); *yahweh* (Jehovah, or "I who am God"); *seren* (used exclusively as the title "princes", "Lords of the Philistines").

"Lord" in the New Testament is used to denote deity. The word *despotēs* ("despot or master") is used for God five times and is translated "only Lord God". The word *kurios* ("lord," "sir," "master") is the major Greek term for both God the Father (see Matt. 1:22; Mark 5:19; Acts 7:33) and for Jesus as Lord or Messiah (Acts 2:36; Rom. 1:4, 14:8; Phil. 2:9-11). The latter verse makes it clear that Jesus the Messiah was exalted to "Lordship" by His obedient death on the cross. *Kurios* is used over 550 times to refer to Christ. Some usages seem to indicate that *kurios,* at times, is used interchangeably for both Father and Son (Acts 1:24, 9:31, 16:14; Rom. 14:11; 1 Cor.

4:19; 2 Thess. 3:16). The significance of *kurios* is that it is the main title used for Jesus, and it means "lord" or "master."

d) "Messiah" (anointed one): the meaning of this term is "anointed to be king." It is a specialized term of kingship. The Hebrew is *māshiah;* the Aramaic is *meshiha,* and the Greek is *christos.* Thus "Messiah" and "Christ" are interchangeable terms. The phrase Jesus Christ is both a name and a title: "Jesus, the Christ." Jesus rarely acknowledged His messiahship because of its strong political connotation. He told only the Samaritan woman, His disciples (upon Peter's confession), and the Jewish High Priest (during His trial) that He was the Jewish Messiah.

e) "Servant" (slave)—*doulos:* Jesus referred to believers as "servants" sixty-two times in His sermons and parables. The book of Acts and the Epistles use the term "servant" thirty times to refer to Christians ("We . . . are servants for Jesus' sake," 2 Cor. 4:5). Every New Testament letter writer called himself a "servant" (Paul, Peter, James, Jude, and John). In Romans 7:6, Christians are instructed to "serve in newness of spirit."

What does the evidence of the Scripture indicate? It clearly shows that "Lord" is the main title of Jesus, and that all of His followers are "servants." He has no "believers" who are not serving Him as Lord.

2. *Salvation and Lordship:* Though men have divided the offices of Christ between Saviour and Lord (as if they were two separate entities), the Bible knows no such division. Jesus is called:

"God my Saviour" (Luke 1:47); "Christ the Saviour" (John 4:42); "Prince and Saviour" (Acts 5:31); "Lord Jesus Christ our Saviour" (2 Pet. 1:11, 2:20, 3:2, 3:18).

The connectives in these phrases clearly indicate that the Saviour and Lord are inseparably one in the same person! When the name of Jesus is used in the appeal for salvation, it always carries the direct connotation of Lordship. As Peter preached at Pentecost, he declared: "Whosoever shall call upon the name of the LORD shall be saved" (Acts 2:21). In the same message he announced: "... God hath made that same Jesus, whom ye have crucified, both LORD and CHRIST" (v. 36).

In recounting the events of that unforgettable week, Luke states: ". . . And the LORD added to the church daily such as should be *saved*" (Acts 2:47). Who is doing the saving? The Lord Jesus (not Jesus the Saviour apart from his Lordship). Peter made it clear to the Sanhedrin that salvation is ". . . by the name of Jesus CHRIST . . . neither is there salvation in any other: for there is none other name under heaven given among men, whereby we must be saved" (Acts 4:10-12). What is that name? Jesus (Saviour), Christ (King), our Lord (Master). The name and title are inseparable.

Paul's testimony is just as clear: "That if thou shalt confess with thy mouth the LORD Jesus, and shalt believe in thine heart that God hath raised him from the dead, thou shalt be saved . . . For whosoever shall call upon the name of the LORD shall be saved" (Rom. 10:9, 13). When asked by the Philippian jailer, "Sirs, what must I do to be saved?" Paul and Silas replied, ". . . Believe on the LORD Jesus Christ, and thou shalt be saved . . ." (Acts 16:30-31).

Writing his last epistle to Timothy, Paul urged him: "Be not thou therefore ashamed of the testimony of our LORD . . . who hath *saved* us, and called us with a holy calling, not according to our works, but according to his own purpose and grace, which was given us in Christ Jesus before the world began" (2 Tim. 1:8-9). Notice again that the Saviourhood and Lordship of Christ are as inseparable as "salvation" and the "holy calling."

3. *Once Lord, Always Lord:* It is certainly true that Christian may sin and that every Christian must ". . . put on the whole armor . . ." (Eph. 6:11); ". . . mortify the deeds of the flesh . . ." (Rom. 8:13); ". . . be filled with the Spirit . . ." (Eph. 5:18); ". . . resist the devil . . ." (Jas. 4:7); and ". . . present [his] body a living sacrifice . . ." (Rom. 12:1).

The Scripture gives many directions to the believer, but NOWHERE is he told: "Now that you have been saved, you need to 'completely surrender' to Christ as 'Lord' of your life." Jesus Himself said: ". . . If any man will come after me, let him deny himself, and take up his cross daily, and follow me" (Luke 9:23). There is a definite experience of daily surrender and of continual rededication to Christ. There is a genuine "growth in grace" and a maturing (or "perfecting") process, but this has nothing to do with making Christ "Lord" subsequent to salvation. This is just as erroneous as the concept that "dedication" is a one-time, secondary sort of blessing that follows salvation.

Jesus Christ is Lord: Lord of Glory, and Lord of the church. When He is received as Savior, He is still Lord. He remains the Lord of the Christian forever, and the believer is always His "servant." When he sins, he is a disobedient servant, but a servant nonetheless. Jesus does not cease to be your Lord or Master just because you sin against His "Lordship." In fact, because He is still your Lord, He will not let you get away with such sin. He will bring conviction and discipline leading to repentance (Heb. 12:6-8).

Two questions need to be clarified here. The first is: Can a sinner be saved apart from acknowledging the Lordship of Jesus? No! The two aspects of Lordship and Saviourhood are inseparable. A proper understanding of this truth would eliminate the cheap, "easy-believe," message of today's preachers. Where there is no godly sorrow over *sin* and resulting repentance, there can be no salvation (see 2 Cor. 7:10). History shows that where there is no strong preaching on repentance and surrender to the Lordship of Christ for salvation, there is no revival. Surrendering to Christ as Lord does not mean that one immediately becomes all that God wants him to be. It does mean that he definitely begins to change (2 Cor. 5:17).

The second question is: What is the Christian instructed to do when he has disobeyed his Lord? He is to acknowledge Christ's Lordship and confess his disobedience. "If any man sin we have an *advocate* with the Father, Jesus Christ the righteous" (1 John 2:1). Our Lord is in heaven pleading His blood on our behalf. Think of it! When you have sinned, you do not need to be saved again, nor make him "lord" again. He *is* your Lord and He is interceding for you. "If we confess our sins, he is faithful and just to forgive us our sins, and to cleanse us from all unrighteousness" (1 John 1:9).

If we are to experience a fresh breath of revival, it will come with the reinstatement of these two vital doctrines. Some may fear that if we preach too strongly on total surrender, we may "scare away" people or "preach Christians into thinking they are lost."

The fear would be valid only if salvation were the work of man and not of God. A well-known preacher, upon hearing of the conversion of one of his staff members replied: "If someone can talk you out of being saved, you never were saved in the first place. I know that I am saved, and no one could ever talk me out of it no matter what he said. It is time we admitted there are lost people even in our fundamental churches. We should stop giving them a false assurance that even the Bible does not give them!"

There are many who desire to be saved from hell and its punishments, but not from sinning. Jesus is more than a "fire escape." He is the Lord of the church. He declared that He "came to call sinners to repentance." Once we have really seen Him and heard Him, we will announce: "What have I to do any more with idols?" (Hos. 14:8)! Then we will cry as did Paul when he *first* acknowledged Jesus: "LORD, what wilt thou have me to do!"

chapter 7

Revival Preaching and Crusades

". . . Striving together for the faith of the gospel."
(PHILIPPIANS 1:27)

In this chapter, we want to consider two different areas of thought: first, the spiritual atmosphere that is necessary for genuine revival crusades; second, the content and emphasis of revival preaching. As we have already stated so many times, the twentieth century church seemingly has lost a great deal of its emphasis upon genuine revival because it has lost the concept of what true revival is, and what it involves. Nowhere is this seen more clearly than in the lives of today's Christians. The apostle Paul urged the Philippian church, "Only let your conversation be as it becometh the gospel of Christ: that whether I come and see you or else be absent, I may hear of your affairs, that ye stand fast in one spirit, with one mind striving together for the faith of the gospel" (Phil. 1:27).

Genuine revival will always unite the forces of truly reborn Christians to work together to spread the gospel of Jesus Christ to an unsaved world. The general qualities of a revival crusade are usually missing from the average "evangelistic meeting" of our day.

Revival Must be Serious

One would think an individual would seriously consider matters which deal with his spiritual and religious development. However, an unreasonable amount of levity and frivolity prevail in many Christian circles today; this attitude is hardly a testimony of the serious and awful truths of the Word of God. All too often, we are attempting to present eternal matters in temporal clothing. Sunday school contests, gimmicks, and promotional enterprises have tended to open the door of the ridiculous into the church service itself! This sad commentary is often true in so-called "revival meetings."

Those evangelists who have never experienced the genuine and powerful moving of the Holy Spirit in their meetings will tend to substitute man-made, synthetic, "religious" experiences for the genuine article. Thus, we have witnessed pew-packing contests, Bible-waving fanaticism, "Jesus cheers," and so on. Because the church has taken such ridiculous steps to seek out today's generation, it has really defeated its purpose. It has alienated itself from any sincere spiritual or intellectual acceptance by that generation. As one studies the history of revival, one fact stands out above all others. When God has moved in genuine revival, it has always come in a state of absolute seriousness. Though humor does have its place in preaching, in the final analysis, a spirit of genuine seriousness must characterize true revival.

Revival Should be Orderly

In writing to the Church of Corinth, the apostle Paul emphasized that "God is not the author of confusion," and that ". . . all things be done decently and in order" (1 Cor. 14:40). Emotional confusion is not genuine revival. Scripture makes it clear that in matters of public worship all things are to be done decently and in order. Now this should not hinder the church or any Christian meeting from the freedom of the moving of the Holy Spirit.

God works with men who are flexible enough to allow themselves to be moved by His direction. Too often we set our time schedule, our dates, and our meetings. In essence, we let the Lord know that we are going to meet at such and such a time on a certain date, and we hope He is going to be there and move on people's hearts; but, if not, we're going to be there with our methods, our programs, and our gimmicks. It is in this attitude that we have lost the genuine power of God in revival. Instead of seeing genuine conversions that last for eternity, we see half-hearted, uncommitted "responses" that are evidence of little more than spiritual remorse. These conversions fall far short of genuine regeneration (Matt. 13:3-23).

The Spirit of God must be free to work in the lives of Christians, unrestricted by clock-watching, materialistic, so-called Christians. It must also be remembered that He does work with a sense of order and direction. Human emotions that would not even be considered decent expressions of concern or commitment in any other course of life, are often proclaimed excessively in religious services. Groaning, shrieking, shouting, individuals speaking simultaneously—all of this adds an element of irreverance and distraction to any service. It takes less spiritual responsibility for individuals to express themselves openly and boisterously in a service than it does for them to genuinely surrender to the control of the

Spirit of God and live a consistent, disciplined Christian life. All too often, the person who shouts the loudest, lives the loosest.

Revival Services Should be Simple

The absence of parade and ostentation is essential in bringing total glory to God. In the Jewish dispensation, there were many things connected with religious worship which were adapted to make a strong appeal to the senses; but all that machinery of religious ritualism was abolished in the New Testament era. Jesus said that the day is coming, "when all must worship God in sincerity and in truth, for the Father seeks such to worship Him" (John 4:23). The ordinances of the New Testament church are simple. The religious expressions of that church are simple and very personal. Whenever the church has lost sight of its mission of truth to each person, the result has always been the amplification of spiritual pride and ecclesiastical complication! The greatest hindrance to genuine revival in the Medieval church was the constant attention drawn from God to men, ritual, form, robes, relics, statues, and architectural monstrosities.

As much as modern evangelical protestants oppose excessive ritualism, we ourselves have often substituted an evangelical ritual of our own. Though more simple, it is just as defined and structured as any other. We have allowed ourselves to become relegated by the clock and by an order of service printed in a bulletin. Moreover, we are reluctant, even afraid, to vary in one degree from that set pattern. Instead of being able to sing, "Like a mighty army moves the

Church of God," we act as if we're singing, "Like a mighty tortoise moves the Church of God, brothers we are treading where we've always trod!" The simplicity of a revival service draws attention to the Word of God, and the Lord of the Scriptures. The great value of simplicity is that it calls all attention away from man, and focuses on the Master.

Honesty Should Characterize Revival

Honesty is the total absence of all worldly artificiality. The younger generation often complains that today's adult world is a "plastic" society in which everything is artificial and unreal. In fact, in a recent advertising campaign, a wellknown soft drink company advertised the slogan: "It's the Real Thing". They even began to print the phrase "The Real Thing" on the side of their aluminum pop cans. However, when one reads the list of ingredients on the opposite side of the can, he discovers the words "made with artificial flavoring and artificial coloring!" We often claim that in Christ we have found the real answer and have the real thing; and yet, upon closer inspection, an outsider may sense in our churches an artificial flavoring that is highly distasteful and disappointing! Honesty is one of the greatest virtues of a mature, spirit-controlled life; and yet, one hindrance to revival is a lack of genuine honesty among professing Christians.

It is true that mere sincerity does not constitute spirituality, because a man may be very sincere about wrong things. Nevertheless, there is no genuine spirituality without sincerity. In accordance with this general concept, every measure which is adopted in bringing sinners to repentance ought to be marked by genuine sincerity. The concept that "the end justifies the means" is destroying today's evangelical church. Many of our ministers have become pragmatists to the point that they say "if it works, do it." The one statement that an evangelist hears over and over is, "Do you get results?" Very few stop to ask, "How do you get these results?"

Overexaggeration of emotional stories or the distortion of scriptural statements to bring results is nothing more than a deceitful handling of the Word of God. Such preachers have approached the Bible as if the Word of God is tame and powerless in its naked simplicity. It is presumptuous for anyone to suppose that God has revealed anything that is not profitable, or that He has omitted anything that is important. God requires His ministers to dispense the word they receive from Him, not to frame His truth in their own relevant expressions. If they will do this, He will take care of the consequences. Much of the exaggerated, excessiveness of modern preaching, results from a preacher's failure to trust in the power of the written Word of God and in the preached Word of God. It is the height of deception to claim that the Word of God is inspired truth used by the Spirit of God to convict men of sin and drive them to the Saviour, and then to feel like one has to supplement its statements with the cleverness of his own distortions.

Honesty in proclaiming the Word of God is essential if God is to move from heaven in genuine revival. God cannot honor lies and distortions of His written truth. Not only is the honest proclamation of the Word of God essential for revival, but so is an attitude of honesty among those who are praying for, and working for that revival. Many a minister has been shocked by the open dishonesty prevalent today among preachers. Dishonesty will cause a preacher to lie about the results of his preaching, the character and quality of his church members, the amount of the offering taken in, and the spiritual results that have come into the lives of those being moved during the "revival."

All men face a constant struggle with pride. It has been our observation that when a pastor's son or daughter is genuinely saved in a revival crusade, pride will often cause the father to be reluctant to admit t! it they have really been saved or even needed to be saved. If the members of a local church resist the Word of God, rebel against it, and fail to ask forgiveness for their sin, the pastor will often justify his people's failures by such phrases as: "Things are different in this part of the country;" "My people are consistent, but they are not used to this kind of open expression;" "Your personality is so different from mine, my people cannot adjust to it;" or "I have to live with this situation long after you're gone." Pride will always cause men to make excuses for sin. Honesty on the part of the evangelist, the pastor, and the people is an absolute necessity to genuine revival. We must be willing to admit our needs. We must be willing to call sin what God calls it. We must be willing to obey every clear principle and direction from the Word of God.

Revival Involves Compassion

The message of the Gospel is essentially a message of compassion. Jesus looked upon the multitudes with compassion because of their situation. Matthew 9:36

tells us, ". . . When He saw the multitudes, He was moved with compassion on them, because they fainted, and were scattered abroad, as sheep having no shepherd."

A genuine and sincere compassion characterized the life of Christ in all of His conduct; in His plea to the city of Jerusalem, and in His tender petition on behalf of His enemies and murderers. The very compassion of His love, however, was often lost among many of His professed followers who were attempting to advance His cause. One reads with great disappointment the record of the religious wars and battles that characterized much of the Lutheran and Zwinglian Reformation. The question often raised in church history has been, what greater effect might Zwingli have had on the Reformed Church had he not been killed in the battle to conquer the city of Geneva?

The clear direction of the Word of God is that we ". . . preach the truth in love . . ." (Eph. 4:15). Such a proclamation of the Gospel is not compromise, but compassion. There is a total difference between preaching love without the truth, and preaching the truth in love. As Sprague himself wrote so many years ago:

> I would have the naked sword of the Spirit brought directly in contact with the sinner's conscience. I would have no covering up, or softening down, of plain Bible truth. I would have the terrors of the invisible Word, and the fearful depravity and doom of the sinner, held up in the same appalling terms in which they are represented in God's Word. But never was there a greater mistake than to suppose that all of this may not consist with an affectionate and inoffensive manner.

The twentieth century has marked the great conflict between liberalism and fundamentalism. Time has now proven the triumph of the fundamental church. However, in the heat of conflict many fundamentalists have forgotten who their enemy is and have begun fighting one another. The ultimate issue involves both love or truth.

The liberals have paraded their sentimental "gospel of love" before a bitter and hateful world that has trampled it underfoot. Meanwhile, some fundamentalists have so hammered the truth that they almost despise compassion for the sinner. God's Word reminds us to "speak the truth in love." God's eternal truths couched in the compassion of the preacher's heart will reach even the hardest sinner.

Revival Preaching

Once the atmosphere of a revival service or crusade has been established by the priorities of the Word of God, it is then essential for the revival preacher to proclaim a message consistent with the goal of revival. The question automatically arises in one's mind: "What is revival preaching?" It is very popular today to use the phrase, "That was a *great* sermon." What do we mean by great? What is great preaching? All too often, "great preaching" is a label given to preaching which is emotionally exciting, humorous, and entertaining. Though the message may contain elements of the gospel, we are inclined to label as "great" that kind of preaching which reflects the unique and unusual personality of the preacher. Often, what is labeled as "great preaching" lacks the solid base and depth of scriptural truth! Great preaching, as far as the Bible is concerned—as far as God is concerned—is biblical preaching. Go to the Word of God and discover His definition of what great preaching really is!

The apostle Paul, undoubtedly recognized as the greatest preacher who has ever lived, tells us plainly in the Bible what "great preaching" really is. He wrote to the Colossian Church, ". . . Whereof I am made a minister, according to the dispensation of God which is given to me for you; to fulfil the word of God; even the mystery which hath been hid from ages and from generations, but now is made manifest to His saints: to whom God would make known what is the riches of the glory of this mystery among the Gentiles" (Col. 1:25-27). Then, after Paul states that he is a minister of the gospel, that the gospel is the mystery which has now been revealed in the New Testament church, he defines what the ministry of preaching ought to involve. ". . . Which is Christ in you, the hope of glory: whom we preach, warning every man, and teaching every man in all wisdom; that we may present every man perfect in Christ Jesus: whereunto I also labor, striving according to His working, which worketh in me mightily" (Col. 1:27-29). In these two verses are given the clearest statement of what great preaching (God's kind of preaching) ought to involve.

1. *Christ-Centered Preaching.* The preaching of the death, burial, and resurrection of Christ must become the core of the gospel message. Gospel preaching, or revival preaching, is therefore Christo-centric preaching. Those who proclaim the Word of God often preach on various side issues which never come to the central message of the gospel—the person of Jesus Christ. These preaching "sidetracts" may include an *extreme emphasis* upon the Bible and science, the dispensations, Bible prophecy, future events,

preaching against liberalism, Communism, and so forth. Preaching on these issues has a valid place in the total preaching of the gospel, but when they become the major thrust of the minister's sermon, he has lost the gospel message itself!

Even one who believes the fundamental issues of the gospel, but does not preach upon the person of Christ is not, by definition, a gospel preacher. The gospel message (the evangel of the New Testament) is the person of Christ. Though every preacher realizes the necessity of preaching "the whole counsel of God," the emphasis of his preaching must be Christ-centered in order for the Holy Spirit to powerfully stir the hearts of people. The greatest weakness of twentieth century preaching is that it is not Christ-centered. It is topic-centered, need-centered, situation-centered, but it is not Christ-centered. It does not emphasize, glorify, and exemplify the person of Christ. Thus, the average Christian has, at best, a weak concept of the person of Jesus Christ. Christ-centered preaching is the answer to the weakness of the twentieth century church.

2. *Preaching Against Sin.* The proclamation of the gospel that meets the need of the sinner and brings conviction to his heart must preach against sin. It has never been popular to preach against sin, and it is even less popular today! Many who have been able to build large churches and establish extensive mass-media ministries have neglected to preach strongly against sin. Throughout Jesus' ministry, it was obvious that His message against sin divided men. Jesus was not one to take the attitude that He should use any method that would "draw and hold a crowd." He often dispeled the crowd that He had gathered by His strong preaching against sin.

Because ministers genuinely love their flock, they

will preach against their sin. Preaching against sin is not preaching against the sinner. It does not involve "fighting" the individual, but rather preaching against the sinful attitudes and actions in his life. The minister realizes that those attitudes and actions are the very things which are destroying him as an individual.

3. *Preaching Involves Teaching.* "And teaching every man in all wisdom." Again, one of the great failures of twentieth century preaching is its lack of doctrinal emphasis. Teaching the whole counsel of the Word of God is essential in the development of the ministry and in effectively reaching the hearts of men. Popular preaching is often so topically oriented, that one may sit through literally hundreds of such sermons without understanding the basic doctrines and principles of the Word of God. Part of the Great Commission is to go into all the world and "teach" all nations. Revival preaching must include doctrinal content that instructs both the unbeliever and believer in his responsibilities toward God.

4. *People-Oriented Preaching.* The goal of great preaching is that we may present every man perfect in Christ Jesus. Many preachers, unfortunately, lose their concern for the individual while proclaiming their message. If one preaches to call attention to himself, to his ability, to his oratory, to his "pulpiteering," he will soon lose the sense of proclaiming the message of God to *people.* People need to be built up and developed in the faith; they need to be matured, completed, perfected by the work of the Spirit in their hearts. A minister should maintain a constant concern for people as "sheep not having a shepherd". The gospel preacher will see more effective results when he preaches to the needs of people, not to an "audience."

5. *Preaching With Effort.* Great preaching involves hard work: ". . . Whereunto I also labor, striving according to His working" (Col. 1:29). One is often humored these days by the advertisements in minister's periodicals for "instant sermons." Preaching the message of the gospel has never been easy. Not only does the preacher need a genuine call from God and the constant empowerment of the Spirit of God, but he also needs to put forth a great deal of personal effort in the presentation of the gospel message.

Anyone who thinks that preaching can be "made easy" has not heeded the clear direction of the apostle Paul. Great preaching always involves great effort and work on the part of the preacher. The amount of preparation in the mind and heart and life of the preacher will determine the ultimate spiritual success of his message. Great preaching must move the heart of the preacher before it can move the heart of the listener. The emphasis of his message must be practiced in his own life. When the truth of the Word of God has moved the preacher's heart and life, then the Spirit of God will use his expression of that truth to move the lives of others.

6. *Preaching With Power.* Great preaching is powerful preaching: ". . . Which worketh in me mightily . . ." (Col. 1:29). Powerful preaching involves preaching with conviction, not just volume. A proclamation of the Word of God that is convincing and convicting will automatically be powerful. The unmotivating message of the average "wilted-lily" type preacher does not have enough power to blow over a tin can, let alone move the life of a hardened sinner or a backslidden Christian!

Men of God in the Scripture and in church history

were powerful preachers like Elijah, John the Baptist, Peter, Paul, John Calvin, John Knox, Jonathan Edwards, George Whitfield and C. H. Spurgeon. These men thundered gospel truths that shattered the resistance of hardened sinners.

The weakness of the today's pulpit can be seen in the weakness of the pew. The average Christian is shallow and indifferent because of the lack of depth and concern conveyed in the average sermon. A lack of power in the life of the Christian layman is generally identical to the lack of power in the life and message of the average preacher. Great preaching, as far as God is concerned, must be Christ-centered: it must involve a warning against sin; it must proclaim the doctrinal truth of the Word of God; it must have as its goal the perfection of the saints. Such preaching requires effort on the part of the preacher. But it is powerful preaching because it is used by the Spirit of God to move the hearts of people. The kind of preaching that God has honored in revival is practical enough to meet the needs of people. It is simple enough for the average person to understand and apply to his own life. It centers about the person of Christ; it is dominated by the power of the Holy Spirit; it is filled with the Word of God; and it moves the life of the preacher before it moves the life of the listener.

chapter 8

Counseling and Revival

"Repent ye therefore and be converted. . . ."
(ACTS 3:19)

Eternity is of great concern to most people. When the sinner's conscience is convicted to the point that he is genuinely convinced of his need to prepare to meet God, he must be properly directed to a genuine relationship with Christ. The sinner is at enmity with God. In no way does his nature seek after, or even lean toward the Lord (Rom. 3:10-12). Therefore, as the Holy Spirit is in the process of developing His work of conviction in the heart of the sinner, he will begin to respond with the question, "Sirs, what must I do to be saved?" Then the person offering counsel and direction must be prepared to point him to the Savior who alone can meet his need. In past centuries, those who were brought to a point of concern for their spiritual condition were called "awakened" sinners. In more current terminology, "awakened sinners" would be those people who are convicted to the point that they seek counsel and direction in meeting God.

Counseling the Convicted Sinner

Care should be taken to note that a person who comes for counseling may not be prepared to give his life to Christ. Many people "come forward" in evangelistic services; but when asked, "Why did you come?" they respond, "I don't know." Although some response is generally a good indication, it may imply an emotional response or an attempt to earn merit with God by nothing more than outward human movement. Therefore, a minister's approach to the "awakened" sinner must be very careful and very scriptural. In the New Testament, when the rich young ruler came to Jesus and said, "Sir, what must I do to meet the requirements of God?" Jesus did not give him a three or four step "quickie" approach to heaven. Rather, He convictingly dealt with the one issue in his life that stood between him and heaven. That issue was his possessions. Jesus told him to go and sell all that he had. The young man went away sorrowful because he had great possessions. Whatever sin the convicted sinner is not willing to give up stands between him and God. It is the "point" of his pride! The counselor needs to realize that God is not concerned about a "decision" written on a card, but a genuine convert whose name is written in the Lamb's book of life!

1. *The Sinner is Guilty.* Show the sinner that he is guilty and will become more guilty in his constant neglect of salvation. The writer of Hebrews asks, "How shall we escape, if we [continue to] neglect so great salvation?" (Heb. 2:3). The Scriptures make the issue clear: ". . . The wages of sin is death" (Rom. 6:23); ". . . The soul that sinneth, it shall die" (Ezek. 18:4); ". . . Sin, when it is finished, brings forth

Glory in the Church

death" (Jas. 1:15). Many sinners contradict themselves by suggesting that their present "personal problems" keep them from repenting and turning to God.

Think of a child who has rebelled against his parents, left town, turned his back on their love and then becomes overwhelmed by a genuine sense of that love; he realizes his parent's concern, but continues to rebel rather than immediately yield to their love. Would it be right for him to add insult to injury? Would it be right for a rebel, urged to throw down this rebellion toward a benevolent Sovereign who genuinely loves him, to acknowledge the reasonableness of submitting to Him in a future day while denying it in the present? Direct the sinner to the realization that continued resistance toward God is the height of unreasonableness! Impress him with his immediate need for repentance, faith, and submission to God. Lead him to throw aside all questions of personal concern and interest and to accept his responsibility before a holy and righteous God.

2. *Today is the Day of Salvation.* Secondly, urge him that the present is the best time for securing his soul's salvation. The greatest excuse in the world is to postpone until the future what needs to be done today. One of the most unusual examples of scripture appears during the time when God used Moses to send ten plagues upon the land of Egypt. One of those plagues was the multiplication of millions of frogs. Though the frogs were a constant nuisance to the Egyptians, they were reluctant to stamp out these "deities." Moses later spoke to Pharaoh and said, "What do you want me to do with these frogs?" His response was, "Get rid of them." Moses then asked the unique question, "When do you want me to get

rid of the frogs?" Pharaoh's reply was, "Tomorrow!" The frogs had been in their houses, in their ovens, and in their beds. He evidently wanted to spend one more night in bed with the frogs! Many people are that way with their problems. They cry out for help now, but when presented with a solution to meet their need, their response is, "I'll take care of it tomorrow; I'd rather spend one more night in bed with my problem."

Help the sinner realize that it is best to respond while the Spirit of God is dealing with his soul. Conditions will be no more favorable for his conversion than those at the present. Dwell upon the appalling fact that trifling with Divine influences will harden the heart. How long does it take for one to harden his heart? The concerned sinner needs to be admonished that he is in danger of losing the serious sense of conviction which he now has. Therefore, he should not consider himself to be "safely" considering his present situation. Caution him against a half-hearted sense of repentance that will only grieve away the Holy Spirit. Urge him to hold God's truth constantly before his mind, so that he may be continually reminded of his opportunity to escape the wrath to come.

One of the most interesting insights in the Word of God is given in the third chapter of the book of Hebrews. In verses 7-8, we read these words: "Wherefore as the Holy Ghost saith, Today if ye will hear his voice, harden not your hearts, as in the [day of] provocation. . . ." The emphasis of this statement falls upon the word "today." Today, if you hear the voice of God, do not harden your heart against Him. How long does it take a person to harden his heart? One day! "Today, harden not your heart." Can one's heart be hardened in only a day's time? Notice also verse 13 of the same chapter: "But exhort one another *daily,* while it is called *today;* lest any of you be hardened through the deceitfulness of sin." How long does it take to harden your heart? Only one day!

Today your heart can be hardened by not responding to the voice of God who is speaking to you right now. As God begins to convict you of sin and convince you of His direction in your life, do not resist what you know to be His genuine guidance. It only takes one day to harden your heart against the Lord. Thus, the sense of present concern and conviction can be lost in just one day's time. However, once the sinner responds to the Saviour, genuinely calls upon Him to cleanse his sin and to change his life, the regenerating work of the Spirit of God becomes permanent, lasting, and life-changing for all eternity!

3. *Salvation by Grace Alone.* Those convicted of sin should also be warned against seeking salvation in the spirit of self-righteousness. Man constantly attempts to control the direction and environment of his life by his own effort. Nothing will lead a person further from genuine salvation than a self-righteous attitude. The young man asks, "What good thing might I do that I may inherit eternal life?" "What can we do so that we can work the works of God?" asks another group. The answer is always the same. "This is the work of God, that ye *believe* on Him whom He hath sent" (John 6:29).

Dr. Sprague points out that we should not discourage the sinner from striving for salvation, but should admonish him to strive in the spirit of the new covenant, not the old. Remind him that there is no merit in any of his striving, and that he can never be saved until he becomes convinced of this. He must fall down helpless at the feet of mercy and be willing to accept salvation as a free gift of God's grace through Christ. The sinner does not earn that salvation. He should be urged to spend a great deal of time reading the Word of God, searching his heart, and spending time in prayer before the Lord.

4. *Salvation from Sin.* The counselor should be cautious to warn the sinner to make conviction, not comfort, his ultimate end. Many people today want to be saved from the penalty of sin, but not from the power or presence of sin. They want to love God and love the world as well. Such a person places himself before God merely as a sufferer who deserves to be released from distress, rather than a sinner who must forsake his evil course and turn to the Lord. God requires repentance, faith, and obedience. Only in this way will the sinner find comfort and peace. He must regard himself first as a sinner, and then as a sufferer. If he genuinely repents from his sin, he has reason to expect relief from his sufferings; but if he holds fast to his sins, he will experience no release, but, ultimately, the wrath of God. Many are seeking an answer to the problems and difficulties of life. They need to realize that the answer is not just in professing Christ as Savior, but in being possessed by Him. When the second person of the Trinity enters spiritual union with the individual, he is always regenerated, changed by the power of God unleashed in his life. When one is genuinely saved, God will see to it that he is no stranger to the joys of His salvation.

5. *The Point of Pride.* The counselor ought to carefully point out any "pride" that might cause resistance to the work of God. Many an unrepentant sinner has cried, as did Saul, ". . . I have sinned, I have sinned . . . but it was not my fault; they made

me do it" (1 Sam. 15:24). Saul's desire to blame his sin upon his people is clear evidence of the fact that he would not accept the responsibility for his own sin.

Some people may take the attitude: "I'll never publicly confess Christ, and I will never verbally acknowledge my sin." Such an attitude reveals a point of pride that may keep the sinner from Christ. The rich young ruler said, "I will not sell all my goods and give them to the poor." Remember, he went away unconverted. In his pride, he willfully rejected total surrender to the Saviour.

Counseling New Converts

Counseling must be directed not only to those who are seeking salvation, but to those who have come to experience the reality of it. The Scripture directs young converts to "prove your own selves . . ." (2 Cor. 13:5). Another of the great weaknesses of the twentieth-century church is that we have not properly dealt with young converts. In an attempt to give them an assurance of salvation, all too often we have left them with assurance of sin, frustration, and failure. Therefore, these next steps that we suggest may seem unusual since they are rarely recommended in the typically quick "one-two-three step" approaches to the unsaved. Nevertheless, they are scripturally grounded, absolutely necessary and essential in producing stability and growth in the life of the young convert.

1. *Make your Calling and Election Sure!* Those who have the hope of eternal life and salvation should guard against an overconfidence in the reality

of that regeneration. The wording of Scripture is "Wherefore the rather, brethren, give diligence to make your calling and election sure . . ." (2 Peter 1:10). Genuine salvation is not evidenced by the emotional quality of the convert, nor by the outward circumstances of his life. Scripture clearly indicates the genuine evidences of true salvation. These must be constantly taught to young converts, as well as to mature Christians who also need to be reminded of God's truths. A genuine Christian will persevere (John 17:12). One need not pray that his decision will "stick," for such a prayer is unscriptural. If his decision is real and genuine, it will stick! The Scripture is resplendent with dozens of *tests* of genuine salvation. The following are some of the more important signs that might be of help to the converted sinner.

a) He has a changed life (2 Cor. 5:17).
b) He hungers for righteousness (Matt. 5:6).
c) He receives chastisement for sin (Heb. 12:6-8).
d) He no longer loves the world (1 John 2:15).
e) He desires to do the will of God (1 John 2:17).
f) He has a new mind of understanding toward the Word of God (1 John 2:20).
g) He does not continue sinning as a normal habit of life (1 John 3:9).
h) He has a new love for other believers (1 John 3:14).
i) He receives genuine answers to prayer (1 John 3:22).
j) He is assured by the indwelling Spirit (1 John 3:24; 4:13).

These evidences do not produce salvation; they are the results of genuine salvation. Spiritual regeneration *always* produces its own fruits and evidences (Matt. 7:15-23). "Salvation" without proof is no salvation at all!

2. *Fight the Good Fight of Faith.* The new Christian also needs to be warned that he has entered upon a course of labor and conflict. It too often appears to the new convert that, having trusted Christ, he has now found release from all of his problems. Any experienced Christian knows that life is still filled with difficulties, but now instead of being overwhelmed by these difficulties, he has a Saviour who can meet his every need. We have discovered the One who is the answer to every problem, but that does not mean that such problems disappear. Satan's constant conflict in the soul of the Christian is very real to the genuine believer. The spiritual struggle between the Spirit and the flesh often will cause a series of "ups" and "downs" in the life of the new Christian. The convert must be cautioned not to be disappointed or discouraged by the conflicts that he faces. He is, in essence, a new baby in God's family, and every new baby must learn to walk. Initially, he will totter and sometimes stumble. But every time he repents and turns to the Lord, God's grace will be sufficient to meet his failure. As he learns to gain stability and maturity in Christian growth, he will be able to walk with greater stability.

He must be encouraged to realize that he is unworthy of the One who has saved him. The labor and trial of the genuine Christian is one of the constant themes of the New Testament. "Fight the good fight of faith . . ." (1 Tim. 6:12); "Put on the whole armour of God . . ." (Eph. 6:11). These are the watchwords of the Scripture. Throughout the centuries the very blood of martyrs became the seed of the church. The apostle Paul once recounted his own experiences: ". . . Five times received I forty stripes save one. Thrice was I beaten with rods, once was I stoned, thrice I suffered shipwreck . . . in perils of waters, in perils of robbers, in perils by mine own countrymen, in perils by the heathen, in perils in the city . . . in the wilderness . . . in the sea" (2 Cor. 11:24-28).

3. *Patterns Begin Now!* The new Christian must be encouraged to realize that the resolutions and principles he adopts from the very beginning will probably set the course of his entire Christian living. Often spiritual success relates most closely to the personal discipline of prayer which Sprague calls the "duties of the closet." The spiritual exercise of personal devotion begins with earnest self-examination. Such examination should be made prior to the communion of the Lord's Supper and should apply to any approach with the infinite God.

Perhaps the major weakness of present-day counseling and follow-up programs is their lack of emphasis on "discipling" converts. The great commission clearly urges Christian evangelists to "make disciples." Yet, the issues of true discipleship are rarely presented to the young Christian who is eager to follow Christ. How often do counselors present the importance of personal Bible study, prayer, meditation, fasting, family devotions, and so forth? The "first-love" enthusiasm of the new believer needs to be cultivated into disciplined Christian living from the very outset.

Young converts should be convinced that all their opinions and principles of conduct must be drawn from the Word of God. This is often the area of greatest conflict in young Christians. Some people begin to throw around their opinions like a sweepstakes winner throws away his money. Every Christian has his personal opinion about various matters relating to the Christian life. The new convert needs to be warned not to seek such personal opinion, but rather the clear direction of the Word of God. He must base every principle of his life upon God's Word; he must center his decisions and opinions upon the Word of God. "Thus saith the Lord . . ." is to be preferred to "This is the opinion of such and such a Christian, or this 'well-known' preacher." If a Christian heeds such a warning in the beginning of his Christian walk, he will avoid a great deal of compromise and confusion. Many new believers, having no such direction, are easy prey to the carnally-motivated ideas often popularized in the so-called Christian press.

4. *Guard Against your Weakness.* The young Christian needs to ascertain his weakness as soon as possible and guard against it. Every Christian soon realizes that he has a "besetting sin" in his life, and it is this weak area that Satan will hit hardest and most often. Again and again, the blow of temptation will fall on one's greatest weakness. Therefore, the new Christian needs to realize, on the basis of his past sinful life, what his greatest areas of weakness are. He must reinforce these weaknesses by the Word of God, by meditation, fasting, and various other spiritual disciplines.

He must also remove himself from temptation. A former thief should not tempt himself by standing around and looking at merchandise which he desires to steal. Rather, he should determine, as much as possible, to stay away from the sources of his temptation. Even though regeneration produces new life and the ability to overcome any problem of sin, the individual still has a "habit-track" that has been reinforced in his life toward his weakness. Therefore, if a man is morally weak in his sexual conduct he will need to discipline his life in that area of temptation. If a man tends to gossip or use abusive language, he may still have a tendency in that direction. A man who has lied, stolen, or cheated may still have a tendency in that direction. The habit pattern of the past must be broken by the power of God and genuine discipline in the life of the believer.

One must be careful, however, not to overcome temptation merely in the spirit of moral self-reformation. The Christian's source of power comes from the Holy Spirit within him. As the apostle stated: "For we know that the law is spiritual: but I am carnal, sold under sin. For that which I do, I allow not: for what I would, that do I not; but what I hate, that I do" (Rom. 7:14-15). Spiritual conflict can only be overcome by the Holy Spirit in the name and power of Jesus Christ who gives us the victory. "Nay, in all these things we are more than conquerors through him that loved us . . . Christ Jesus our Lord" (Rom. 8:37ff.).

Finally, admonish the young convert to beware of the world. The onset of victory in any conflict is the ability to recognize the enemy. Throughout the history of Israel, one of God's unusual methods was to confuse the enemy to the point that they annihilated one another. In the confusion of battle, many a soldier has failed to identify his enemy. Unfortunately, many Christians have fallen the same way. In an attempt to live for the Lord, to defeat sin and temptation, they have forgotten their real enemy:

116   *Glory in the Church*

Satan and the world! A great hymn asks: "Is this world a friend to help us on to God?"

The ungodly world system must be recognized as the enemy of the Christian. Thus, the Word of God reminds, "Love not the world, neither the things that are in the world . . ." (1 John 2:15). Love of the world and envy of worldliness are the greatest sins of the Christian. How can we envy that from which we have been saved! How can we turn our backs on a loving and just Saviour who died for our sins? He allowed Himself to be nailed to the cross for our sin, and then, in essence, reached out those nail-pierced hands to express His love toward us! Paul admonished Timothy, ". . . Let every one that nameth the name of Christ depart from iniquity" (2 Tim. 2:19). The young Chrisitan should be urged to keep his distance from the world, not to live as close to it as he would.

The "church triumphant" of the last days must be a godly one. She must be a bride prepared and spotless. She must lay aside the garments and trappings of sin that taint her appearance. When the unsaved attend a church service, they do not come to see their people and to hear their music. They know that their way of life is empty and vain. When they see so-called Christians who look, talk, and act like the unsaved, they will not see a spiritual beauty that they should desire.

Pastor, realize that the lost come among your people in search of a holy life. The unsaved do not come to see how much like them we have become. "If *my people,* which are called by my name, shall humble themselves, and pray, and seek my face, and *turn form their wicked ways;* then will I hear from heaven, and will forgive their sin, and will heal their land" (2 Chron. 7:14).

postscript

The Story of the Lynchburg Revival

October 7-19, 1973
by Dr. Jerry Falwell
Pastor, Thomas Road Baptist Church
Lynchburg, Virginia

Prior to October 11, 1973, I must confess that I had never witnessed a real revival. Since that time, I have seen several outbursts of glory in our church and schools. Like many of you, I had read the account of the Asbury revival, *One Divine Movement.* My heart cried that God might give "another divine movement" for our students. But I am convinced that many of us are not experiencing genuine revival simply because we do not know what revival is.

Let me share with you the first experience of revival at Lynchburg. Our church is know throughout the world for its ministry and evangelistic, soul-winnig efforts. Yet, prior to the Autumn of 1973, we had never experienced the power of revival. On the seventh of October, the Life Action Crusade team from St. Petersburg, Florida, arrived at Thomas Road for a scheduled week-long evangelistic crusade—or so I thought. Under the direction of Evangelist Del

Fehsenfeld, Jr. and Dr. Ed Hindson, this unique group of young adults began sharing a message of revival with our people.

At first the meeting began slowly, but not without significant blessings. On Sunday night, the seventh of October, Del preached his oustanding sermon: "Phoney Baloney Christians." Over fifty people were saved that night, including many professing Christians. Our youth director, Rev. Vernon Brewer, immediately came under deep conviction about the assurance of his own salvation and gave a public testimony the following night of God's dealing in his life.

On Monday morning, during the chapel service for the Lynchburg Baptist College, Dr. Hindson preached on "Ten Evidences of Salvation", and several more professing "Christians" were genuinely saved. Like the preaching of young Jonathan Edwards during the Great Awakening, these two young men kept hammering at the evidence of change that ought to characterize genuinely reborn believers.

During the week, the meeting progressed with a quiet awesomeness. On Tuesday night Ed preached on "Revival in the Family" and over one hundred families publicly committed themselves to a regular time of family devotions. As a pastor I was amazed and deeply concerned to discover how few fathers were actually leading their families in regular family devotions. On Wednesday night, Del preached on "Having a Clear Conscience with God and Man." Attendance numbered 3,500 and the power of God was overwhelmingly evident in the service. However, during the invitation for people to clear their consciences with one another, something seemed to stall the earlier conviction. Perhaps the size of our auditorium made it difficult for people to find each other in the crowd.

The events of Thursday, however, convinced me that the size of a church is no deterrent when revival comes from God. God doesn't care whether he is working with just three or three thousand. From a human standpoint, I am sure we all left Wednesday night a little discouraged. Yet, the Holy Spirit's conviction was still heavy upon ever heart.

During the school day on Thursday there were no scheduled chapels. The Life Action team gathered off campus for a time of soul-searching, prayer, and fasting. Then, totally unknown to our church staff, something began to happen. The Spirit of God, almost mysteriously, began to overwhelm students in our academy. A high school student suddenly burst into tears and asked to be saved right in the classroom. A teenager from another class went to the principal asking him how to be saved. Soon, spontaneously and totally unrelated, dozens of students came under such intense conviction that many classes had to be turned into counselling rooms. Our principal, Vern Hammond, reported to me that, "School has been called off in favor of God!" Before the day was over nearly fifty young people had been gloriously saved.

The crowd came in Thursday night totally unaware of what had happened earlier. There was no sermon preached at all in the service. Prior to the scheduled message, the opportunity was given for people to share a brief testimony of what God was doing in their hearts. The response was tremendous. Dozens of young people and adults testified to God's working in their own lives and their families. After an hour of testimonies, an invitation was extended to those with whom God was dealing to go to the prayer room to meet alone with God. Ninety-nine people were saved that night!

Later that evening, Dr. Ed met with students in the lobby of the hotel (our downtown dormitory) for the nightly "rap session" and prayer meeting he had been conducting with our students. Over five hundred students crammed into the lobby. Kids were sitting on the stairways, table tops, everywhere. The "rap" time was set aside for a prayer meeting. The students joined hands and began to call on God for revival. Again a deep sense of conviction came over our college students. Several left the prayer meeting to pray to God. Only the record books of heaven know how many were saved that night. Several were still being counselled at 2:00 A.M. when the prayer meeting closed with the singing of "Jesus, There's Just Something About that Name."

Afterward several individual student prayer meetings continued throughout the night. Spontaneous singing and weeping could be heard all over the dorms. Yet there was not one incident of extreme behavior. By Friday morning the entire church and campus were electrified. Classes went on as usual until the 10 o'clock chapel service. Again there were testimonies from the students, and again God moved. Several students quietly left their seats and made their way to the prayer rooms. The chapel service lasted two and a half hours. For the second day, the school schedule had been interrupted in favor of revival.

I had never before seen anything like it. I had read about revivals of the past, but until that week I had never really seen one. Our staff met with the Life Action directors and the decision was made to continue the crusade until God was finished working. We were ready to cancel everything in favor of God.

On Friday evening, during the early part of the service, the Life Action singers presented their multimedia school assembly program on drugs and suicide.

A thirty-two-year-old housewife raced out of the auditorium under conviction. One of the girls from our Chorale followed her and led her to the Savior. Later Ed Hindson preached again. I had rarely seen two men share the pulpit with the graciousness and effectiveness of Del and Ed. The message on the "War with Russia" could not have been more timely. Israel and Egypt had just renewed a fresh conflict that very week, and God used this to bring a renewed awareness of Christ's return. Another hundred, this time mostly adults, were converted that night. The prayer rooms were packed, tears were flowing, and everywhere people were smiling and praising God for what He was doing.

I began to observe one of the major characteristics of a revival: when it starts, you cannot stop it! People were reluctant to leave the service. They seemed to want to bathe in the atmosphere of God's Spirit. More spontaneous prayer meetings were starting in homes and throughout the dorms. That night nearly one thousand students went to pray at the hotel and the Treasure Island dormitories.

Several students, in light of Christ's immanent return, were deeply concerned for unsaved loved ones. Many called home long distance and led their parents to Christ over the phone. Some even drove home to urge their families to trust the Saviour. One young seminary couple drove twelve hundred miles home to win the wife's father to Christ. Suddenly there was a burst of soul winning among our students such as we had never before experienced and which still has not stopped.

Students went everywhere throughout Lynchburg witnessing the gospel of Jesus Christ. During the weekend God continued working. My office was constantly filled with people wanting to be saved. On Sunday morning the church was aflame with the glory of God! The air of expectancy rung with congregational singing that sounded like the choirs of heaven. During Sunday School, we dispensed with the lesson to allow adults to share their testimonies. Some were married students, some laborers, some professional people, some were converted "church members," some had never been in church prior to that week.

Every testimony rang with a clear expression of God's grace. No one was self-righteous nor questionable. Again, God moved. Dozens of people were saved. So many were coming under conviction that our "timing" was totally thrown off for our television broadcast. We went on the air with tears in our eyes. God was unbelievably at work in His church! The sacred atmosphere of the morning carried over into the television broadcast. People later wrote from all over the country to ask what God was doing.

A few testimonies were given in the church service, and, after delivering a brief message on revival, I invited those who were lost to come to the prayer rooms. They began coming from every direction. People of every age and rank in life were being touched by the Holy Spirit. The service went on for two hours. Up until then, 323 had been saved, and before that morning was over, about 250 more had been born again!

The nightly services continued throughout a second week with people being saved every night. After thirteen continuous days of services, 683 had been saved, and nearly everyone was baptized. In the four-day period from Thursday through Sunday, there were nearly five hundred people converted. God had visited the Thomas Road Baptist Church, and truly, it was an experience of "glory in the church."

That was not to be our last touch from heaven, for our revival never ended even when the Life Action team went on its way. Time and time again, we were to see outbursts of revival in our church services and college chapels. I have learned some significant facts about revival during this past year. First, you cannot start it without God. Secondly, if God is in it, you cannot stop it when it comes. Thirdly, you cannot keep it going when He has decided to quit!

"Revival" means to stir afresh that which is already alive. It increases our devotion to our Lord Jesus Christ and our efforts to get the gospel to the lost. God has given me the responsibility to use the ministries of our church, schools, and the "Old Time Gospel Hour" broadcasts to call America to revival. We need an old-fashioned, heaven-sent, Holy Ghost revival in our homes and churches!

Our Lord has put us here to glorify Him, and it is only as a revived and quickened people that we can truly glorify Him. May the Holy Spirit bring such a sweeping sense of conviction over our churches that He brings us to real repentance, confession, and humiliation before God. In a time of national despair, David cried: "Wilt thou not revive us again: that thy people may rejoice in thee?" (Ps. 85:6).

I feel the church has lost its sence of revival and its "ministry of rejoicing" for three reasons. First, most of us are prejudicial. Our hearts are fixed and our minds are set. We have prejudged (this is the real definition of prejudiced) people, the potential for revival, and the purpose of God for these last days. We must learn to forgive everyone. Our conscience and heart must be cleared. We desperately need an open mind so that God may do a new thing in our midst. We must not crowd Him out with prejudicial thinking.

As stated before, unconfessed sin is certainly a second and tremendous hindrance to revival. We must be willing to be honest and fair with ourselves and others. Finally, there is little revival and rejoicing because most of us are not living by faith; therefore, we have little contact with supernatural happenings. We are generally caught up in this automated age that is geared to planning and programming. Even in our ministries, we have unwittingly ruled out the spontaneous working of God's Holy Spirit in our lives. Most of our tragedies and troubles are God's way of pressing us to the life of faith. Once we learn to trust God implicitly, we immediately see God move in mysterious and supernatural ways in our behalf. Nothing brings praise and revival to an individual, a family, or church than miraculous answers to prayers and supernatural interventions from heaven.

The curse of America is religion without repentance. Our churches are filled with people who have never repented of their sins. You can join the average church more easily than most civic clubs. For that reason, we desperately need an invasion from heaven which only a revived and praying church can effect. But when God moves on the scene, the impossible happens rapidly. Nothing is too hard for the Lord. Let us set our faces toward God and claim revival in our time.

The glory of God is one of the grandest themes of the Bible. In Revelation 15:8, we read that His glory fills the heavenly temple. In Exodus 40, God's radiant presence filled the tabernacle in the wilderness. Later, His glory was minfest in Solomon's temple (1 Kings 8). After the constant sin of Israel, God withdrew His glory (gradually) from that temple as Ezekiel records in the eighth chapter of his prophecy. When a second and then a third temple were built, there was no record of that glory returning. Not until several hundred years later would a choir of angels on a hillside near Bethlehem proclaim: "Glory to God in the highest, unto you is born this day a Saviour." In the person of Jesus Christ, the personfied glory of God returned to earth. The apostle John said of Him: ". . . And we beheld his glory, the glory as of the only begotten of the Father . . ." (John 1:14). Jesus came from the glory of heaven to the midnight of earth that He might establish His presence (His glory) in the church. It is our prayer that God will move in revival among His people in such a way that "glory may dwell in our land" (Ps. 85:9)!

Dr. Ed Hindson addressing 3,000 member LBC student body in chapel

Student praying during Lynchburg Revival

Mother and sons reconciled

           Nightly student prayer meetings

Evangelist Del Fehsenfeld, Jr.

Dr. Jerry Falwell

Spontaneous student prayer meetings